ACTING YOUR INNER MUSIC

Music Therapy and Psychodrama

Joseph J. Moreno

MA, MME, MT-BC

MMB MUSIC, INC.

ACTING YOUR INNER MUSIC
Music Therapy and Psychodrama

Joseph J. Moreno, MA, MME, MT-BC

Cover art: Pablo Goldenberg
Figure illustrations: Amanda Rice
Editor: James H. Heine
Typography: Gary K. Lee
Printer: Publishers Express Press, Ladysmith, WI
1st printing: October, 1999
Printed in USA
ISBN: 1-58106-012-2

For information and catalogs contact:

MMB Music, Inc.
Contemporary Arts Building
3526 Washington Avenue
Saint Louis, MO 63103-1019 USA

Phone: 314 531-9635, 800 543-3771 (USA/Canada)
Fax: 314 531-8384
E-mail: mmbmusic@mmbmusic.com
Web site: http://www.mmbmusic.com

To my dear parents, William and Anne,
whose love knew no boundaries

Contents

Preface

Only You Know What Is in Your Heart
—Shona song, Zimbabwe

I have been involved in integrated psychodrama and music practice since the mid-1970s. J. L. Moreno and I discussed these ideas as early as the 1960s, and he was extremely receptive to the innovative possibilities. Far from seeing his own work as a cultural conserve to be perpetuated in its original form, he was open to new directions and innovations. He welcomed creative thinking and actively supported new directions, techniques, and applications of psychodrama. I have always thought of psychodrama as something far more significant than a therapeutic method, limited to dealing with problematic situations. Rather, it has far greater significance as a path toward a more creative approach to life from which all people can benefit.

The essential goals of psychodrama are to enable people to develop in spontaneity and creativity, which are often diminished in those who are suffering from significant emotional problems and tend to become withdrawn. There is some irony here, in that when confronted with serious problems, at exactly the time when the healing inner resources of spontaneity and creativity are most needed, it is precisely when these potentials are least drawn upon. This is where psychodrama can play a special role in helping to access and make the best use of these resources.

Moreover, few people are always functioning at their optimum levels of spontaneity and creativity. Therefore, participating in psychodrama at any time, at any level of participation, whether in an active way as protagonist or auxiliary, or even just as an involved observer who can learn from the protagonist's experience, all can benefit, and at any point in their lives. If it is necessary to provide just a single rationale for the integration of music and the other arts into psychodrama, it would be that these added dimensions can enhance the impact of the psychodramatic experience and maximize the possibilities of stimulating the spontaneity and creativity of the participants.

BECOMING A DOER

The following story (not apocryphal) beautifully illustrates the basic psychodramatic concepts of spontaneity and creativity:

It was New Year's Eve, some years ago, in a crowded restaurant in New York. The party included J. L. Moreno; my father, William Moreno (a brother of J. L.); an actor, Walter Klavun, who was associated with psychodrama in the early years; and others. All of the group were becoming increasingly impatient and annoyed, as they were being ignored by the busy and distracted staff and not getting any service. All were hungry, with no food at the table, and still hadn't even been able to place their order.

Finally, Klavun, the actor, who had excellent social skills, engaged one of the waiters. While discreetly slipping him a hundred dollar bill, he began to negotiate for food and service. As this negotiation proceeded, the existential situation remained unchanged, i.e., no service, no food. At this point, and without announcement, my father got up from the table, walked directly into the kitchen, filled a large serving tray with food, and brought it back to the table to serve the hungry and appreciative group.

J. L.'s response to this was to exclaim, "There's the difference. Klavun is an actor, and William is a doer!"

The message here is that we should all be "doers" in our lives. That is, to not spend too much time negotiating or intellectualizing, but rather to do, to act, to become the best that we can be. To become a doer in life may not always guarantee a desired result, but it does mean that you will be living fully, in true response to the moment, and in harmony with the biblical golden rule that urges us to "do" unto others, that is, not merely to reflect, but to take positive action.

A memorable session I once conducted exemplified the idea that in psychodrama insights realized through "doing" often help to realize far more profound kinds of insights than those derived from assumptions arrived at internally and untested by action.

The protagonist in this session was a young woman involved in a romantic relationship that was highly gratifying. The single flaw she was experiencing in the relationship was her concern about its future direction, as her boyfriend was unable to make a clear commitment to a shared future with her.

We first explored some representative scenes in her relationship, in which she and her boyfriend (played by an auxiliary) argued about this critical issue. The auxiliary played the role of the boyfriend very well, expressing things such as,

"But ———, why the pressure? Why can't you just appreciate and enjoy what we have right now? What's your problem?"

All of this seemed right on target, and the protagonist affirmed that this was exactly how things were between them, the very opposite from what she wanted, which was a clear future with marriage at the top of her agenda.

For the following scene, I took the auxiliary boyfriend aside and told him to replay the same encounter with her, only this time to give her everything she said she needed from him. On their return, the boyfriend was transformed. He expressed things such as, "I've been thinking about us, and I've been a total fool. You're the very best thing that ever happened to me, and I don't want to lose you. Let's stop putting things off. I want us to get married, and right away. Maybe we can even do it tomorrow!"

However, instead of the joyful response from the protagonist one would have expected, she appeared to be completely disconcerted. She blushed, and her response was, "Tomorrow? Isn't that a little quick? What's the big rush?"

In this scene, having been given all that she thought she wanted, she was forced to acknowledge that what she had so wished for wasn't what she wanted after all. It had been easy for her to project her own relationship ambivalence onto the boyfriend, and by having chosen a relationship with a man who couldn't commit himself, she had conveniently avoided confronting her own problems in this area. In the magic of psychodrama, a kind of protected reality in which all things become possible, she was able to experience what she had hoped for, through action. Through the living and "doing" of it, she clearly learned that the problem was not with the boyfriend, but rather it resided within herself. Without this experience she could have continued to delude herself indefinitely. Psychodrama was able to reveal what her previous psychotherapy had not.

 Psychodrama is a uniquely holistic therapeutic method that has virtually unlimited potential for integrating all of the arts—drama, music, art, and dance. Although psychodrama is most often thought of and practiced through enactments that primarily revolve around verbal interaction, this is not an inherent limitation, and certainly not what was intended by its creator. On the contrary, Moreno had the greatest possible breadth of vision, and was always interested in and experimenting with ways to expand the psychodramatic process. His early experiments with what he termed "psychomusic" are well known (Moreno, J. L., 1964), as well as his association with pioneering dance therapist Marian Chace. Others have since developed various techniques for integrating art into psychodrama, such as Bingham (1970), all of which reflect the rich possibilities of integrating the creative arts into the psychodramatic method. Further, as this book will demonstrate, the arts in psychodrama can be used simultaneously and in various combinations, all, of course, extending the therapeutic possibilities for participants in this work.

The approaches presented in this book are intended to have broad applications. In different ways, they can be utilized effectively by music therapists, psychodramatists, art therapists, dance therapists, psychologists, psychiatric nurses, counselors, and others involved in group therapy work.

Music therapists are not trained in psychodrama and should not attempt to carry out psychodrama sessions in the clinical setting. However, this does not preclude them from adapting some of the many musical psychodramatic techniques described here and implementing them in their music therapy sessions. Such techniques as musical role reversal, musical mirroring, musical modeling, and others utilizing psychodramatic elements are very accessible. These can enable music therapists to add new dimensions to their work without overstepping the professional boundaries of psychodramatists.

In analogous ways, psychodramatists are not trained in music or music therapy and therefore cannot undertake to engage in music therapy clinical practice. However, they can still make effective use of many musical psychodrama processes, as adjunctive techniques, to enhance their principal work as psychodrama directors. Many of the music techniques described here are improvisation-based and do not depend so much on a formal music background as they do upon developing specific kinds of musical sensibilities and understandings. Improvisation as an approach is a key—and unifying—element that is common to both music therapy and psychodrama.

The performance of composed music can be seen as directly analogous to the performance of a play in the theater. In both instances, the challenge for the performers, whether musicians or actors, in Mozart or Shakespeare, is primarily to interpret and assist in the realization of the vision of the creator. Therefore, while interpretive tasks may certainly draw upon inner resources to some degree, these kinds of performances are not essentially personal revelations.

By contrast, music improvisation as utilized in musical psychodramatic work, is an intensely personal and revelatory expression, just as playing roles in psychodrama is equally personalized. This common element of personally expressive improvisation in both music therapy and psychodrama allows for a wonderful integration through which the participants can truly *act their inner music*.

As Carolyn Kenny (1976) eloquently stated regarding her work with children, developing an understanding of music that is expressed in projective music improvisation requires "listening to music in a different way," and how "In a very certain situation, that music can be more moving to me, more beautiful than any music I've heard by famous composers, simply because I've developed a relationship with the child, and I hear what the music is saying, what it's telling me," and "As a music therapist every sound means something, every silence means something."

Art therapists can draw upon some of the music techniques described here to stimulate their clients in new ways, dance therapists have the same kinds of possibilities, and there are potential applications for others involved in group therapy work.

Finally, in the best sense, I hope that this book can lead to more frequent interdisciplinary collaboration between therapists of differing orientations. Music therapists and psychodramatists can work together to realize psychodrama sessions of great power, and this can be further enhanced by the collaboration of art and dance therapists. There is no reason for the creative arts therapies to be practiced in isolation from each other, and their integration can realize new therapeutic possibilities for clients.

When psychodrama is integrated with music, the result is a hybrid form that is distinct from its sources. What occurs is an indivisible union of the two modalities, something more than when psychodrama is practiced separately. It is certainly a form of psychodrama in that all of its traditional elements remain intact; yet it is also a form of music therapy since music plays an intrinsic role in the therapeutic process. The resultant combination of music and psychodrama might best be termed *musical psychodrama*. Musical psychodrama can be defined as the integration of music improvisation, imagery, and other music therapy techniques with traditional actional psychodrama, in order to realize an expanded approach that transcends the possibilities of either method used separately.

If this book should stimulate any therapists in initiating collaborative work with colleagues from differing orientations, particularly between music therapists and psychodramatists, and inspire any readers to become more creative doers in their lives, then my efforts will have been amply rewarded.

*Where are all the inner musics
waiting to be heard, visions struggling
to be born, boiling energies held
deep within? What contains us
and holds us captives even
while we are free? How can we
break these chains?*

*Let us sing as the birds do, see
the world as children in all of its
myriad rainbows of brilliant
colors, act in harmony with our
deepest feelings, and live fully
in the true spirit of creation.*

—Joseph J. Moreno

Chapter 1

Music Therapy and Psychodrama:
Complementary Therapies

If a man does not keep pace with his companions, perhaps it is because he hears a different drummer. Let him step to the music which he hears, however measured or far away.

—H. D. Thoreau
Walden

Music therapy and psychodrama are very distinct therapeutic disciplines, with obvious differences, and yet they share many complementary affinities.

Music therapy has been defined by many professional associations, with varying orientations, from around the world. Therefore, a single definition of music therapy that would be universally accepted remains elusive. However, most would agree on some general principles, most certainly regarding the central role of music in the therapeutic process. For example, Bruscia's definition (1989) states that "music therapy is a goal-directed process, in which the therapist helps the client to improve, maintain, or restore a state of well-being, using musical experiences and the relationships that develop through them as a dynamic force of change."

In this definition, we can identify some of the factors that are normally considered essential in music therapy practice. These include a goal orientation, as well as the concept of well-being, that suggests a holistic and indivisible continuum between mental and physical health without artificial divisions. This broad definition of health provides implicit recognition that music can affect a broad spectrum of psychological and physiological parameters. Finally, this definition places the appropriate emphasis on the primary role of music experiences, and the relationships that develop from them, as the essential factors in realizing positive change.

Some music therapy research has sought to separate the effects of the music in therapy, as distinct from the context of its presentation by the therapist. In practice, these factors are generally inseparable from each other, as well as from the reciprocal interactions that involve the therapist and the individual client or group receiving this therapy.

Psychodrama, the therapeutic method created by J. L. Moreno in the 1920s, has been defined as "the method by which individuals can be helped to explore the psychological dimensions of their problems through the enactment of conflict situations, rather than talking about them" (Blatner, 1988).

Just as music is essential to the music therapy process, dramatic enactment is an essential part of the psychodramatic experience. Psychodrama enables participants to move beyond the usual limitations of therapies that are confined to undramatized verbal dialogue. Through the liberating experience of dramatic enactment, the psychodrama stage provides an action-oriented yet protected reality, in which problems can be dynamically explored with the support of a director and group.

In what ways are these two disciplines complementary?

A primary connection is that music therapy and psychodrama are both action methods that directly involve clients as active participants in their own treatment. The client in music therapy who is musically improvising his or her feelings on an instrument as an alternative to verbal expression, and the protagonist in a psychodrama who is assuming roles and interacting with auxiliaries, are obviously actively involved. Even the client in music therapy who is silently participating in a music and imagery session, showing no overt response, may be deeply involved in the experience at many levels, just as a silent member in a psychodrama group may be vicariously absorbing and learning from the experiences of the protagonist. These latter examples are not at all passive responses. Rather, they reflect a different kind of inner-action that may lead to more overt participation at a later time.

If less precise than verbal communication, music is a language of its own that is an alternative and equally valid form of expression. Morley (1981) suggested that "music is a form of communication analogous to speech in that it has cadences and punctuation." Aldridge (1996) took this a step further, questioning the too often accepted primacy of language over music, by posing the reverse idea, that language should be seen as a form of music. Perhaps of more significance than attempting to determine which of these forms is primary, music or language, it would be more helpful to recognize that these are simply alternative forms of expression that can meet changing needs at different times. In the context of the integration of music and psychodrama, these alternative and complementary forms of expression are both made fully available to the participants in a setting in which they can switch between verbal and music expression as needed.

Condon (1980), in studying the micromovements of persons in conversation, determined that when listeners are fully attending to what is being said, they are actually moving in rhythmic synchronicity with the speaker. In effect, there is a conversational rhythmic dance taking place that may represent a form of communication that is more basic than the verbal content being expressed. This connection is a form of rhythmic entrainment, the common pulse that can develop between objects that are vibrating in close proximity to each other. Therefore, it follows that effective communication is correlated to a rhythmic connection. This would suggest that by introducing the musical element into psychodrama we can even further enhance the communication between the participants. In musical psychodrama, music often serves to support and mirror the verbal interaction. In this way, the protagonist can be musically supported while at the same time engaging in verbal exchange, thereby making it possible to even more deeply bind the rhythmic entrainment. In effect, speech and music, taking place concurrently, maximize the participants' rhythmic connections and may have a positive effect on degrees of involvement and communication.

There has been a tendency for music therapy to be subsumed under the umbrella of other therapeutic frameworks. For example, this has involved the use of music as a contingency in behavioral frameworks, in an analytic context as associated with the work of Mary Priestley (1985), and in conjunction with many other therapeutic orientations. In all of these meldings of music therapy with other therapeutic models, the integration of music has added new dimensions and creative possibilities to these approaches. Many music therapists have expressed concern that, in this way, some of the unique aspects and identity of music therapy, as an independent discipline, were being lost in the process. However, within the integrated processes of music and psychodrama presented here, a variety of recognized music therapy techniques are utilized that operate on their own terms. Without compromising their integrity, such methods as projective music improvisation and music and imagery are fully realized. At the same time, new and integrated techniques are introduced that seem to inseparably combine elements of both music therapy and psychodrama. These include techniques such as musical mirroring and musical modeling, and many others, that are both intrinsically musical and intrinsically psychodramatic.

If we define music therapy in the broadest sense as occurring in any therapeutic intervention in which music plays an intrinsic role, then it is certainly taking place in the processes of musical psychodrama.

Music and drama are deeply connected, culturally and historically, both in relation to the essential role of these combined modalities in the venerable world traditions of music and healing, as well as through the close ties of music in support of theatrical forms such as film, dramatic theater, opera, and many others. These close affinities between music and drama, both in healing and in theatrical forms around the world, make a strong case for bringing these two disciplines together in the context of modern clinical practice in psychotherapy.

Music therapy and psychodrama both support the development of spontaneity and the uninhibited expression of feelings. When integrated in musical psychodrama, they can realize new and extraordinary therapeutic possibilities.

Chapter 2

The History of Music in Psychodrama

I feel that from now on, music should be an essential part of every analysis. This reaches the deep archetypal material that we can only sometimes reach in our analytical work.

—C. G. Jung

In Psychodrama (Moreno, J. L., 1964), Moreno described his early experimentation with music in psychodrama. While not formally educated in music, his creative vision instinctively recognized the power of music and its potential within the psychodramatic context. He called his approach "psychomusic," through which he intended to remove musical expression as the exclusive property of musically educated elite performers, thereby returning the creation of music to the majority of persons who, in Western culture, most typically relate to music in a passive and nonparticipatory way. Moreno wanted music to become an active, that is, creative function in the life of ordinary people, and through this realize "a return to more primitive ways which probably have been in operation at the cradle of musical experience" (Moreno, 1964). Moreno suggested two forms of psychomusic, first what he termed the organic form, that is self-made music without musical instruments, relying on the body, i.e., vocal music and/or rhythmic expression. Since most musical instruments suggest, or require a level of skill to achieve self-expression, he saw them as barriers to musical spontaneity. Second, he proposed the use of musical instruments, but he approached them in a way that allowed for free expression rather than forcing the individual to be intimidated by the instrument's history and potential in the context of formal music-making.

As an example of the first organic approach, Moreno presented his idea for a musical warmup, in which the director creates and sings short melodic fragments to the group, supported by rhythmic movements. The purpose of the warmup is to stimulate the group to a state of freely producing vocal music responses. At the right moment, the director would call upon a potential protagonist to begin to enact real or imagined situations, in typical psychodramatic fashion. The verbal dialogue in the session was then replaced by short sung exclamations, with the director encouraging the now musically warmed up audience to echo each sung phrase, like a chorus.

This approach seems to have had the value of energizing the protagonist and the rest of the group and generally stimulating group spontaneity and catharsis. While this could have been an effective warmup, it did not involve a further exploration of the potentials of musical warmups to reach the deepest kinds of issues for psychodramatic exploration. However, it is important to realize that Moreno's experiments in this direction took place in the 1930s or '40s, at a time when music therapy was just beginning in the United States. Therefore, he had no models of music therapy to draw from, and his ideas about music were certainly forward-looking in his time.

To realize his ideas about instrumental psychomusic, Moreno attempted to create an impromptu orchestra composed of six members from the New York Philharmonic. Here Moreno speaks about instrumental music expression in the formalized sense, implying musical and instrumental mastery that can only be realized through years of disciplined practice. Considered from that perspective, he was right in suggesting that sophisticated and self-expressive instrumental improvisation on the usual orchestral instruments is out of reach for the musically untrained. However, in general, he was not correct in stating that "only men who master their instruments are capable of spontaneity work." It is now standard in many music therapy approaches to encourage spontaneous music improvisation for all types of clients, not only for the musically untrained, but even for those with the most severe handicaps, such as autistic children, the multiply handicapped, and others.

A special consideration in improvisational music therapy is the choice of instruments. Moreno was working with performers on orchestral instruments, which, in fact, do not easily lend themselves to spontaneous musical expression with musically naive persons. However, in this context, music therapists usually rely upon a variety of percussion instruments, such as xylophones, drums, bells, gongs, rattles, and other similar instruments that lend themselves to immediate and spontaneous musical expression for any person, whether musically trained or not.

In fact, in work with music therapy improvisational techniques, it is very often the case that musically trained participants are less musically spontaneous than musically untrained persons. This is because extensive musical training often conditions musical performers towards expressing the musical conceptions of others, a form of musical re-creation, rather than towards original creation, an expression of the self.

This problem of the loss of musical spontaneity for musically trained persons is often a barrier to completely free improvisation, particularly in personalized and improvised musical expression that is unrestricted and without considerations of tonality. By contrast, the musically naive person is generally not inhibited by such barriers. In Moreno's work, he made use of symbolic scenarios in an attempt to inspire his classically trained musicians to create more spontaneously, but the connection between this and actual psychodrama work is not made.

Moreno also described, in considerable detail, his work with a 45-year-old man, a violinist and concertmaster of a major orchestra. He suffered from severe performance anxiety that manifested itself in hand trembling in his public performances with the orchestra, and particularly in solo passages.

He did not have this trembling problem when playing alone, or in front of his wife and students. However, in the highly visible role of concertmaster, he was extremely aware of the judgments of his musical colleagues, and of the audience, which distracted him from expressing the music in a relaxed and spontaneous manner. Moreno was creative in his approach, asking this man to approach his playing in new ways, such as playing the violin with an imaginary bow, playing the bow on an imaginary violin, or pantomiming the playing altogether with an imaginary instrument. He was able to accomplish this without trembling, and it was an important first step in his musical spontaneity training.

The next stage involved the patient in real playing on the psychodramatic stage, at first in front of small groups of friends, and then, through a gradual process of desensitization, before more people, including strangers. Finally, Moreno attempted to reduce the anxiety that performers often feel in face of the responsibility towards particular musical works that are recognized as "great" music, and the resultant sense of obligation to the composers, by encouraging the patient to create his own music, to improvise. As a result of these sessions involving musical pantomime, gradual desensitization by performing in front of increasingly larger and less familiar audiences, and then focusing on improvisation rather than on composed music, the patient became increasingly confident, and in this context his trembling ceased.

Finally, in a transition to the real professional performance situation, Moreno used the technique of encouraging the patient to focus on positive imagery. This imagery was intended to be developed while practicing at home, with the goal of carrying over that imagery into the orchestral reality. The specific focus of the imagery was intended to encourage the patient's spontaneous love for the music, and to try to encourage and separate this spontaneous response from the conditioned response to great music as a cultural conserve. Ultimately, the violinist made great progress and was able to achieve musical successes that were fully recognized and appreciated by his peers.

Moreno's ideas were quite creative and effective in this case, and he demonstrated a real sensitivity to the kinds of problems that afflict many performing musicians. While interesting as a case of music therapy, Moreno did not fully utilize music as an integral part of his psychodrama work. However, his creative approach opened the door for others to develop what he had initiated.

This idea of "playing" an imaginary instrument reminded me of a memorable psychodramatic evening at the Moreno Institute in New York in the 1970s. Before a session had begun, the late Hannah Weiner, a brilliant director, asked me, as a pianist, to perform something for the group as a kind of warmup. Although I usually have some degree of performance anxiety myself, I was happy to oblige that evening, the only problem being that there was no piano in the theater. However, as that is really only a minor concern in the world of psychodrama, I accepted, walked onstage to great applause, and seated myself in front of the imaginary piano.

When the audience became silent, I began to "play." However, I didn't simply pantomime the physical movements of playing. Rather, I performed and clearly heard each note, in this case the first movement of the Clementi Sonata in F-sharp Minor, Opus 26. This is a wonderful work that I had been studying at the time, and I played with deep concentration and musical feeling, inspired by the rapt attention and "listening" of my audience. When I concluded the piece, I received a standing ovation, as well as an imaginary onstage bouquet. In fact, this was one of my great musical experiences and perhaps my best realization of that piece. In this context I was able to fully realize my ideal conception of the Clementi work, from beginning to end, and without the constraints normally dictated by flesh and keys and hammers and strings.

Although at the time it was not intended for that purpose, this kind of musical "performance" can provide good role-playing experience for musicians with performance anxiety, and "playing" in this kind of protected reality can build confidence towards preparation for real public performance situations. This was certainly anticipated by Moreno in his work with the violinist, and that evening's performance remains with me as a special psychodramatic moment.

It was during the 1970s that I frequently attended the public psychodrama sessions that were held at the former Moreno Institute on Manhattan's West Side. These sessions were a notable social experiment in themselves, with different psychodrama directors assigned to direct on different nights of the week on a regular basis. These sessions were open to a walk-in public, and any interested persons could attend and participate for a nominal cost. As a result, the institute sessions became a true theater of life, temporarily bringing together entirely random mixes of people. The sessions were endlessly fascinating, unpredictable, and often volatile, in which anything could happen (and often did!).

In attending these sessions and participating in auxiliary roles, I became particularly interested in the dynamic qualities of those playing the roles of psychodramatic doubles. The double's task is to become an extension of the protagonist, to become so psychologically entrained with the protagonist's feelings that they can help protagonists better express themselves. For example, a good double can be intuitive enough to sense when protagonists are holding back on overtly verbalizing a strong sentiment, something they may have a real need to express towards auxiliaries playing the roles of significant others in their lives.

The role of the double becomes critical at these moments, particularly when strong and confrontational feelings may be boiling in the protagonist just beneath the surface. If the protagonist needs to express an aggressive and therefore sometimes difficult feeling such as "I hate you!" the protagonist can be emotionally liberated if the double is able to intuitively anticipate that need and initially say it *for* the protagonist. At that moment (assuming the double has correctly intuited the protagonist's true feelings), this exclamation can then trigger the protagonist into his or her own expression, i.e., "That's right, I *do* hate you!" and so on, opening the door of repressed emotions.

In these kinds of interactions, it's not just the double's words alone that stimulate the protagonist into verbal expression. Rather, their full impact largely depends upon *how* this verbal stimulus is presented; that is, the degree of emotional intensity and volume, the quality of the sound. Stated softly, flatly, and literally, the same words would not realize the desired effect.

In observing the most dynamic and talented doubles in those years in New York, I often noticed that in the most dramatic and emotionally charged moments, the doubles would seek out any possible means of additional sound reinforcement to add to the energy and power of their words. They might spontaneously stamp a foot, or occasionally fling a folding chair across the highly resonant wooden psychodrama stage, which would make a sudden jarring and crashing noise. These dynamic sound stimuli, instinctively created by the doubles in the heat of action, resulted in a kind of implied musical support. The bang of a stamping foot, or the crash of a chair flung across the stage were nothing less than percussive musical sounds, with the purpose of further energizing the protagonist, using the stage as a drum. In fact, the entire circular and highly resonant traditional wooden psychodramatic stage can itself be seen as a kind of symbolic drum, with all the participants as musicians bringing the drum to vibration and life.

My own feelings were that if doubles seemed to spontaneously seek out and try to create sound reinforcements in their work, an implied symbolic music, then there was no reason not to proceed to the next logical step and explore the possibilities of purposefully introducing real, live music into psychodrama. From these beginnings was born the idea of musical psychodrama. It should be noted here that the basic idea of musical reinforcement for the double is not only applicable for volatile moments in a session, but it can be equally effective in supporting poignant moments such as the expressions of feelings of love, pain, or grief. In such moments, as will be explained and illustrated, music can be equally effective.

By enlarging upon preexisting potentials that are inherent within the psychodramatic method, it becomes possible, with music, to realize a psychodrama of new and even greater possibilities of therapeutic power, for the benefit of those who are fortunate enough to participate in this process.

Chapter 3

Music in Psychodrama:
Basic Processes

The core of musical psychodrama is a psychodramatic musical improvisation ensemble. The role of the ensemble is to create, at any given moment, improvised music to support a wide variety of emotions. These musically expressed feeling states must communicate effectively to all participants in the psychodrama. Although the range of human emotions is great, the musical representation of these emotions may be cast into some broad and representative categories. Such emotional categories may include sadness, anxiety, terror, joy, fear, peace, longing, nostalgia, melancholy, and so on.

The musical devices for expressing these kinds of basic emotions are already well established in Western culture. In composed music, slow tempi, soft sustained sounds, and a tendency toward minor modalities are often associated with sadness and related introspective emotions, while major modalities, bright tempi, shorter phrases, and greater volume are typically associated with more positive and dynamic feelings. Some of these elements can be drawn upon for ensemble improvisations in musical psychodrama, although most often the music will be a completely free kind of sound expression without any modal, tonal, or other formal musical constraints.

For purposes of intragroup communication, rapport, and immediate responsiveness to the director, the improvisation ensemble drawn from the participant group should not be larger than six to eight music-makers. The group must work together, with the director, to achieve a consensus concerning the musical means to communicate these feelings. The basic ensemble approach generally involves totally free atonal improvisation, focused upon conveying the desired emotions through effective sound expression. Although major and minor modalities may come into play incidentally, no conscious use of tonality is employed. The most effective musical expression is achieved through group training that emphasizes the musical characteristics of various emotions, rather than specific musical devices. The ensemble functions best with sensitive participants from the psychodrama group, whose degree of spontaneity and lack of inhibitions are far more important considerations than prior music education or other traditionally valued musical skills.

Instrumentation for the improvisation ensemble can vary widely, but some variety of sound color is essential. Various untuned and tuned percussion instruments are basic, and these would typically include metallophones—which may be tuned pentatonically or in modal scales—gongs, bells, rattles, drums, individual tone bars, tambourines, and others to create the broadest possible variety of sonorities (see fig. 1).

Even a highly skilled composer would have difficulty composing music to definitively convey fine distinctions between emotions, if the music was heard apart from its dramatic context or program. As an example, a great deal of programmatic music with accepted imagery might not convey the composer's intent when performed for an audience unfamiliar with the program, but seems to fit when the program is known, such as Tchaikovsky's *Swan Lake* or Smetana's *The Moldau.*

In a similar manner, in musical psychodrama, the listener becomes predisposed to respond to the music emotionally in association with the dramatic content of an enactment. Within a psychodramatic enactment, when improvised music is being played sensitively to support a dramatically expressed action, it is generally perceived by the protagonist, and other participants, as expressing precisely the designated feeling.

The improvisation ensemble is not limited to instrumental sounds, but may also use vocal sounds, as well as singing or toning. Raised voices can increase the emotional impact of the musical sounds of anger and chaos, while crying or moaning sounds can enhance the poignancy of instrumental sounds of sadness. The total possibilities of sound that can be created by the ensemble are used in this way to express emotions, and to support and guide the protagonist.

Live and improvised, rather than recorded and composed music, is essential to achieve flexibility. Improvised music can move with the client, from moment to moment, and match or influence his or her constantly changing feelings. If composed music is familiar to the client, it may elicit a previously learned emotional response rather than a response that is appropriate to the client's present emotional state. Since improvised music elicits no specific associations with the past, it has the potential to reach the client at the deepest and most spontaneous emotional level.

In one-to-one or small group music therapy, a single music therapist can use improvisation effectively to enhance nonverbal communication. For instance, the Nordoff and Robbins approach (1977) focuses on keyboard improvisation to initiate and maintain communication with autistic and emotionally disturbed children. However, some practical difficulties are inherent in this approach. Many

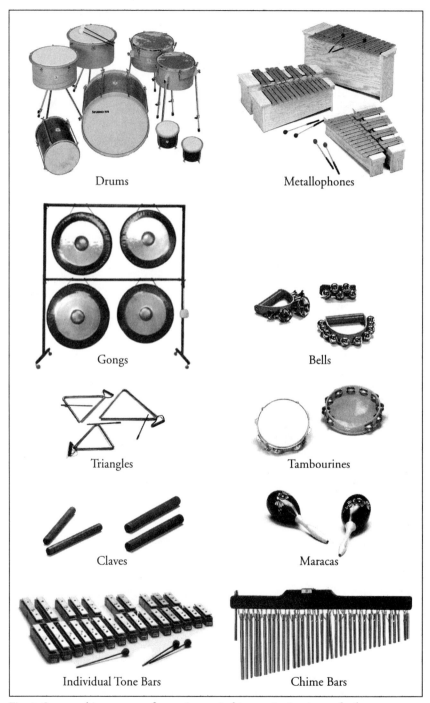

Fig. 1. Suggested instruments for use in musical improvisation in psychodrama

otherwise musically competent therapists may not have the range of keyboard improvisatory skills sufficient to employ this approach effectively, and these possibilities would be completely unaccessible for the musically untrained. This challenge becomes even more significant when attempting to adapt the principles of the Nordoff-Robbins approach to work with adult patients in group therapy.

The use of an improvising musical ensemble, as in musical psychodrama, has many advantages. The ensemble has a far greater range of tonal variety and dynamic impact than any keyboard player, and the individual performers need not have any trained musical abilities. Even the modest abilities found in the participants in any psychodramatic group can realize a workable ensemble, in which their collective musical impact can compensate for individual lack of musical training and can provide effective group musical support.

The ensemble musicians are cued by the psychodrama director. With an experienced ensemble, all that may be needed are nonverbal cues or brief whispered asides such as "anger" or "sadness" or "build tension" in combination with the use of traditional cues to indicate crescendos and diminuendos, entrances, or cutoffs. This cuing may be entirely silent, the director guiding the music with the appropriate body language, and this can be critical during highly sensitive moments when audible cues would be distracting.

The music-makers in the improvisation ensemble should be placed so that they are always in direct visual contact with the protagonist and the director. Their roles are not limited to that of a rigidly seated ensemble, and they should be allowed to move around the stage, performing at different locations or directly following the protagonist when appropriate. Many psychodramas will follow the warmup period by leading the protagonist in a soliloquy, supported by the director. This dialogue will enable the protagonist to provide further details about whatever issues he or she raised in the warmup, and that will now be explored in the session. This information will be important for the director and for others in the group who may later be called on to play auxiliary roles.

Since the soliloquy is often revealing, it is understandable that some protagonists may be inhibited in making this level of disclosure in front of a group. Most protagonists manage to do this, particularly when working with a warm and supportive director. However, even in the best circumstances, some protagonists may find this initial exposure difficult and threatening—and at a point that generally occurs well before they are fully involved in the session.

At this stage of a psychodrama, music can play a significant and supportive role. As the protagonist begins to disclose about different personal issues in the soliloquy, the director can call upon the music group to create improvised music that matches the character of the feelings being expressed. If the feelings are sad and introspective, then a soft, gentle, and almost subliminal music can be played, music that will be more felt than consciously heard.

Like the music used in trance induction in healing rituals, this is not music to be attended to. Rather it is music for the purpose of helping protagonists to stop attending, to let go, and to immerse themselves in the psychodramatic reality. I have directed many sessions in which the music, introduced at this stage, seemed to pull the protagonist into the enactment and remove any barriers of self-conscious inhibitions. What the music actually provides is a unique form of supportive communication between the whole group and the protagonist. Empathy is being communicated through this personalized music, and it is delivered in a continuous, audible and nondistracting manner, *concurrently with the protagonist's verbal expression.*

This process is entirely different from what can occur in even the most supportive verbal group therapy setting. That is, in the verbal group, when an individual has something difficult to express, he or she must first speak without any direct evidence of group support and then wait for the anticipated verbal expressions of approval and acceptance. With the use of supportive improvised music in psychodrama, as has been pointed out, there is virtually no delay between the verbal expression and the empathetic support. Rather, these are both realized simultaneously, and the entire group can communicate this musical support at the same time, rather than individually, as is normally the case in verbal expression. Of course, even in musical psychodrama, verbal support can also be realized later in the session. However, group musical support provided at this early and critical stage is a wonderful way of drawing the protagonist more deeply into the psychodramatic process.

In analogous ways, it is possible to simultaneously support movement or artistic or musical expression itself with improvised music. However, in utilizing improvised music to support verbal expression in psychodramatic enactments in an ongoing way, we are realizing a kind of music psychotherapy that retains and parallels the verbal interaction characteristic of most psychotherapeutic interventions.

Salas (1996) has worked with music in the psychodramatically related form of Playback Theatre. Salas is a trained music therapist, in addition to her primary involvement in Playback Theatre, and has made music an essential part of the Playback experience. In Playback, the primary function of music is to support the emotional impact of the performances. However, much emphasis is given to the role of a competent musician as an important part of the Playback company. Since Playback is often performed by a group of actors, for the benefit of the participants, it follows that the music is primarily presented for, rather than performed by the participants. Also, while the music in Playback is generally improvised, it seems to draw from conventional musical idioms to support the theatrical action, rather than the more fundamental kind of freely improvised music that is associated with music in psychodrama.

In musical psychodrama, the music is created entirely by the participants. Further, although music, in the more conventional sense, can sometimes serve the theatrical function of supporting the action in psychodrama, it also has much broader applications. Through a variety of techniques, the music in psychodrama becomes intrinsically bound to the entire process, from warmup through closure.

Despite all of the potential inherent in the integration of music in psychodrama, it should also be kept in mind that music, as with any other medium, can be overused. If music is too constantly present, it can become distracting and begin to lose its impact and value. However, if made use of with sensitivity, creativity, and discretion, and introduced at the right moments, it can become truly magical.

Chapter 4

Music Improvisation Warmups

Mary Priestley, the noted British music therapist, is the originator of analytic music therapy, an improvisation-based projective technique that is defined as "a way of exploring the unconscious with an analytical music therapist by means of sound expression" (1985). Analytic music therapy techniques can be freely adapted to serve as psychodramatic warmups.

To begin with, the therapy setting must be provided with musical instruments. As has been suggested previously, a variety of percussion instruments is generally most appropriate, typically including drums of various types and sizes, tambourines, bells, rattles such as maracas, gongs, metallophones (metal xylophones), individual metal tone bars, and others (see fig. 1). Some simple wind instruments such as recorders can also be included.

There are several distinct advantages in using tuned and untuned percussion instruments. Most important, they do not require any prior musical experience whatsoever to achieve immediate sound production. Because of this, they lend themselves easily to free improvisation techniques as a form of personalized projective sound expression. A special advantage of untuned percussion instruments such as drums and gongs is that they avoid the often confining tendency inherent in instruments with harmonic possibilities, e.g., the piano or guitar, of somehow suggesting a diatonic improvisational style with chordal accompaniment. This is a conditioned approach that many people intuitively bring to these familiar instruments—instruments which should be avoided in this work. Such diatonic melodic improvisations can become the musical equivalent of superficial and stereotyped verbal expression, rather than a profound inner projection, since these kinds of musical expressions are learned rather than spontaneous, more external than internal.

The goal of these projective music improvisation techniques is to encourage an honest expression of feelings through a direct and uncluttered means.

Untuned percussion instruments, like drums, gongs, rattles, and tambourines, or single-pitch instruments like metallophones, bells, or tone bars are often the most effective for this work since most group members will probably have had little or no active prior experience with them. They are therefore likely to elicit spontaneous expression. In this kind of projective improvisational technique, the ideal way to approach these instruments is as a child would, in play therapy, as a medium for free and relatively unconditioned expression.

As noted earlier, it is interesting that musically naive persons are often freer in this than people with formal musical training, who often find it difficult to be spontaneous in this way and to escape from the strictures of their musical conditioning. This is reminiscent of a statement attributed to Picasso, to the effect that all his life he had tried, but was never able to draw like a child. To express adult feelings through these instruments, with the spontaneity of a child, is the goal of this kind of music-making.

Warmups are a critical part of every psychodrama, serving to energize the group and helping to identify potential protagonists with issues that can be explored in psychodramatic enactments.

Chapter 5

Individual Music Improvisation

To initiate this warmup, the psychodrama group should be seated in a circular or semicircular formation, with the musical instruments spread out on the floor in the center.

A subgroup of five or six participants is asked to volunteer or is chosen by the director, and each is encouraged to select their preferred instrument for the stated purposes of self-expression. Then each group member is asked to create a solo improvisation on their instrument, expressing how they are feeling at that moment or how they are feeling about their overall life situations. These improvisations should then be tape-recorded for subsequent playback and group analysis.

This kind of musical improvisation warmup is an effective projective technique, and even the simplest improvisations can be highly revealing of various feeling states. Through experience in listening to these kinds of expressions, it becomes possible to recognize the various kinds of feelings projected through the musical statements.

Fig. 2. Music improvisation group for warmup experiences

Points to look for when listening to these improvisations can include the following:

1. Dynamic considerations are always significant. Is the music generally loud or soft, and how do these dynamics correlate with the individual's general affect? Of course, "loud" and "soft" are relative considerations, but here we are looking towards extremes in either direction, and particularly in terms of how these dynamics might be contrasted, at different times, in the musical expression of a single individual. Strong contrasts might reflect inner divisions, conflicting issues that an individual may be dealing with.

2. Does the music have a continuous and flowing quality, or is it characterized by breaks and abrupt changes of character? Does it seem organized or chaotic?

3. Does the music convey a feeling of direction, confidence, and determination, or does it sound weak and apathetic?

4. Like dynamics, considerations of tempo, while also relative, can be very revealing. If at all rhythmic, does the music convey a fast movement, or is the expression slow and funereal?

5. How does the individual approach the instrument? Does he or she creatively explore the potentials of the instrument, making good use of its space (as on a large drum head), as well as its sonorous possibilities? Is the person inhibited, taking only minimal advantage of a potentially strong and expressive instrument?

6. Does an individual's improvisation sustain the same characteristics over a period of time in therapy, or are there changes that are evident? What are these changes, and how might they reflect ongoing changes in the person's life situation?

7. What about the duration of the improvisation? Is it relatively extended, and therefore potentially revealing, or is it obviously terse, perhaps suggesting a fear of dealing with a difficult issue?

Of course, in this context we have to develop a different sense of what we mean by "music." That is, we must learn to hear and to perceive "music" in the broadest sense of sound expression, and this requires a great deal of experience in order to develop a new kind of listening, musical sensitivity, and perception.

Even the group members' initial choices of instrument can be revealing. As an example, the choice of a large drum over a small rattle may be directly related to the kinds of feelings the individual feels motivated to express. Of course, this is not always directly correlated, in that a large drum may be played in a soft and introverted way, and a small rattle loudly and aggressively. Equally significant is an individual's pattern of choice of instruments over time in ongoing therapy groups.

The taped individual improvisations are then played for the group and discussed and analyzed by the director and the group members. The group members are each encouraged to try to determine the feeling state of each person as expressed in their improvisations. The director must make it clear that these are not to be judgments, but only perceptions, to be expressed in tentative terms such as "She seems ambivalent, the character of her music keeps changing" or "His repetitive banging on the drum seems to be expressing a cry of pain." After some time devoted to this kind of group discussion, the individuals who created the improvisations are then each asked to verbally clarify the feelings expressed in their music to the group. In this way, all potential problems of the subjective judgments of others are eliminated, as it is the individuals themselves who finally explain the nature of their musically projected feelings to the group.

Quite often the group will be very sensitive and intuit the specific character of the musically expressed feelings correctly. At the same time, this discussion serves as a catalyst to further clarify and support the expression of each individual's issues. In any case, even if the group's perceptions would prove to be entirely inaccurate, this can often serve to stimulate the individuals to even more strongly own their feelings, and to assert the "correct" interpretation. This could be something such as "No, I'm not sad, I'm really very angry, but I'm too scared to let it out." In fact, occasionally the director might intentionally choose to *misinterpret* an improvisation, just for this reason. That is, after an obviously tense improvisation, the director might say "Well, you sound pretty calm today" for the very purpose of having the potential protagonist respond with something like "No, I'm not calm at all! I'm incredibly tense about everything these days." Of course, the director will pick up that cue with "Well, what are you so tense about?" and a session has begun.

It should also be kept in mind that not every improvisation will be reflective of a problem. If an improvisation sounds playful and positive, it may well be just that, and nothing more, and the therapist should not be overly motivated to look for hidden meanings when none may exist. In general, the individual's self-description about the music should be taken at face value.

In some instances, even when the therapist may have strong intuitions that question the validity of these verbal explanations, and it appears as if there is a strong contradiction between what a person plays and how they describe their feelings, it could be counterproductive or even harmful to confront the patient about this directly. A person will disclose their feelings when they are ready and able to, and any strong contradictions between the music and the described feelings will probably also be obvious to the individual at some level. This insight may well serve to warm up a person to greater self-awareness—and to further disclosure at a later time.

The ultimate purpose of these individual improvisations is not only to develop group listening, focus, sensitivity, rapport, and disclosure, but also to identify the individuals in the group with the most pressing issues to serve as psychodramatic protagonists. Group discussion of individual music improvisations is a fascinating process, and group members often become deeply involved in an intense kind of attending to the subtle relationships and nuances that exist between sound and feelings. Because of the newness of these kinds of musical experiences, these sound expressions may be attended to with great interest by all members of the group. In fact, it often happens that the level of attention, group listening, and mutual group sensitivity evidenced in these improvisation experiences far surpasses what typically occurs in verbal group therapy processes.

In one memorable session, a single improvisation became the genesis and leitmotif of an entire psychodrama. A woman in the group expressed herself forcefully on a small gong in the individual improvisation warmup. The group perceived her expression as agitated and fearful, and she confirmed this as accurate. Her fear was of physical pain—not pain she was experiencing at that moment—but anticipated pain that might occur in the future.

I told her that I, who was directing the session, was a doctor and specialist in pain removal, and what was obviously called for was immediate psychodramatic surgery to remove her fear of pain.

Surrounded by a group of auxiliaries playing the roles of doctors to assist in the operation, she was told to lie down, close her eyes, and try to imagine the worst possible pain she might have to face. The six auxiliary doctors sat around her, each with a musical instrument of the kind used in the musical warmup.

As the protagonist described her pain, I encouraged her to be as specific as possible. She characterized her pain as "sharp and agitated"—which, in fact, was very similar to the character of her initial gong improvisation.

The medical auxiliaries first attempted to musically match the character of the protagonist's pain, to express its agitated and intense qualities through intense and strident musical sounds. The protagonist was told that the music would at first reflect the intensity of her pain, and that it would then gradually soften and become less intense. She was told to try to imagine her pain as gradually diminishing, and finally disappearing when the music stopped.

When the music gently ended, she opened her eyes and appeared much more relaxed. She stated that she felt much less scared of this imagined pain than she had been. At that moment, I had her face a prepared auxiliary who played the personified role of her pain, and I told her that now she had to gather her courage and verbally confront her pain. She had to tell the pain auxiliary that she was no longer afraid of her, and once and for all say good-bye to this pervasive fear.

The protagonist was terrified of the pain auxiliary and was totally unable to face or address her. I then asked several of the other auxiliaries to verbally model for the protagonist and confront the pain auxiliary in an assertive way. In spite of this strong modeling, she still couldn't face her pain. Finally, I asked her if she might find it easier to confront the pain auxiliary with a musical instrument, rather than with words, and she agreed to try this. She again chose the same gong she had used in her initial warmup, and for the first time looked directly and defiantly at the auxiliary of pain. She then struck the gong with an enormous intensity, and at the same moment she summoned all her courage and dramatically cried out "Good-bye!"

In this example we can see how music improvisation was used as the initial warmup, with the protagonist's agitated gong sounds directly expressing her anxieties. Later, her description of the agitated quality of her pain in the psychodramatic operation matched the character of her original gong improvisation. I next used the technique of music-mediated imagery (Rider, 1987), musically guiding her imagery from focusing on her worst imagined pain to moving to the point of releasing it.

Finally, she again used the gong sounds for re-warming herself up to confront the pain auxiliary in the final scene of her session. In effect, she had provided her own musical double with the gong, and this gave her the dynamic impetus she needed to say good-bye to her fear of pain forever.

Another memorable experience related to the use of individual improvisation as warmup occurred with a woman who had been a participant in a workshop that I conducted in Switzerland. This woman selected two instruments for her improvisation, a small xylophone and a drum. Her music improvisation was starkly divided, and she created two very polarized musics on the two instruments. On the xylophone she played very soft, warm, and flowing melodic lines with a tranquil quality, and this was alternated with very abrupt and violent outbursts on the drum, followed by returns to the melodic xylophone music. The contrast between these two expressions could not have been more striking, and suggested that these were a reflection of some marked inner divisions.

In fact, her particular life situation was highly polarized. On the one hand, she was married to a highly successful businessman, and in her marriage was often obliged to be his companion in social situations with his business colleagues, playing the role of the happy and perfect wife. This incongruent and superficial role was what she expressed on the xylophone.

However, there was a far darker shadow side to her life. She had been living with cancer with an uncertain prognosis, was not happy in the marriage, and was also dealing with an alcohol problem. It was obvious that the abrupt drumming episodes were an expression of this darker side. The ensuing discussion led her into a psychodrama in which all of these issues were explored, and at the close she indicated that she had made some progress in coming to terms with these various problems. After the session, I had no reason to assume that I would ever see her again.

Two years passed, and I found myself conducting another psychodrama group in Italy. To my great surprise, one of the participants in the group was the same woman from the Swiss group. Again, I utilized the same individual music improvisation warmup, again she volunteered to participate, and once more she chose the same instruments she had previously selected, a xylophone and a drum.

What was immediately apparent to me about her new improvisation was that it was, in some ways, remarkably similar to the improvisation of the past. However, it was also far more tranquil with much less of the anguish that had been so evident before. The soft xylophone playing was reminiscent of the earlier session, but the drumming episodes seemed far less frequent than I remembered. They were relatively subdued, as if only a distant echo of her past anguish. As she explained it, and later dramatized in her psychodrama, many of her past issues had been largely resolved in the intervening two years. Her marriage had improved and she was able to communicate with her husband on a more genuine level, her cancer had gone into remission, and her drinking problem was under control.

This did not mean that her life had become an ideal one, or that some of her earlier conflicts had been entirely eliminated, but rather that her overall situation had greatly improved. What was particularly fascinating in this case was how her improvisation, separated by an interval of two years, directly correlated with the changes in her life. The same polarities still existed, but had been largely reduced, and much had been resolved. The choice of the same instruments, two years later, clearly mirrored the fact that remnants of the prior inner division were still with her. However, her progress in dealing with these conflicts was expressed in her far less divisive musical expression.

It should be kept in mind that while all such analyses of musical expression through projective improvisations are certainly subjective, this does not in any way detract from the value of this technique in terms of its effect of focusing the group and leading to issues for enactment. Clients in therapy may become jaded over time in fully relating to the verbal expression of feelings, and, as has been suggested, in the musical improvisation group they may well focus far more intently than in verbal therapy. Making a real effort to try to sense the meaning of feelings expressed through this symbolic musical language is a challenge, and this striving to feel, understand, and empathize with what others are expressing and experiencing has real therapeutic value in itself. Often the group is quite sensitive to what is expressed through these musical projections and is able to interpret the individual's feelings accurately. What we are dealing with here is the art, not the science, of music therapy. Since in all cases the individuals themselves will clarify the precise nature of their projected feelings, the accuracy or inaccuracy of interpretation ultimately becomes a secondary consideration.

Aside from the information that is symbolically projected by individuals through their music, there are always other cues that enhance the group's ability to interpret musical messages. If the group members already have significant information about an individual's life situation, e.g., that a person is anxious or depressed or angry, then that will certainly color how they interpret what they hear. The individual's body language also becomes a visual cue, in which things like facial expression and general demeanor can also color the way the same sounds are perceived. At the same time, in a general sense, even if these kinds of improvisations were tape-recorded and played for a group that had no prior knowledge of the people involved, many of the same conclusions about the nature of the musically projected feelings would be surmised, even without visual clues. It can be helpful for the therapist to maintain a sound log of an individual's music improvisations to see how these musical statements correlate with progress, or lack of progress, in therapy.

In all of these situations, it remains critical to always allow the individual improviser to have the final word and to make no assumptions without seeking this kind of validation. Even cultural differences can greatly affect both the subjective meaning of an improvisation and the way in which it is perceived or misperceived by others in the group.

I recall presenting a workshop in South Africa in which I made use of the individual improvisation technique for purposes of a psychodrama warmup, and a particularly interesting and culturally revealing experience centered around a group improvisation exercise. Each member of the group was asked to individually improvise on a musical instrument of their choice, to try to express their general feeling states. The other group members would try to intuit the feelings being expressed through the improvisations, and then the individual improvisers would verbally clarify their intentions.

One African man in the group chose a drum, and his improvisation consisted of a very extended and regular moderate tempo rhythmic pattern. The group members perceived feelings such as a clear sense of direction, determination and so on. Finally, when the man was asked to verbalize his feelings, he said that he had been drumming to summon the ancestral spirits! Nothing could have more dramatically exemplified how culture can influence musical perceptions and the differences between Eurocentric and Afrocentric responses to the same musical stimulus. This certainly points to the very real problems that must be overcome in trying to apply music therapy on a universal basis, defining principles that go beyond culture-bound assumptions.

These individual music improvisation techniques are a wonderful resource for music therapists, psychodramatists, and others involved in group therapy work, serving as an excellent bridge towards opening up group sensitivity, and easily leading to the revelation of important issues for use in psychodramatic explorations.

Chapter 6

Group Music Improvisation

The same group formation can be used here as in the individual improvisation techniques, in which a subgroup can be selected out of the larger psychodrama group, ideally involving five or six persons. The emphasis here is on collective or group improvisation. As in the individual improvisation technique, each member of the group is asked to select a single instrument from the available selection, whichever seems to attract them or feels most comfortable. It is very helpful in this approach to have only one instrument of each kind available for selection, each with distinct timbres, so that in the subsequent playback of the group music it becomes easier to identify the musical role taken by each group member.

After all participants have selected their instruments, the director asks the group, at will, to begin their improvisation, which they are told will be tape-recorded. The director should clarify to the group, in advance, that there are no conditions on the length or brevity of the improvisation. This is entirely the group's prerogative. Any individual, or more than one person, can initiate the music, as well as lead the group to closure. Each group is unique. Even with the identical instruments, no two groups will produce the same music, and even the same group members will create different music with each successive improvisation experience. These group music improvisations provide a wonderful and special way of looking at group processes from a very different perspective than the more usual verbal group therapy context.

Once the improvisation begins, the director should remain silent until the music reaches its complete ending, which will be signaled by a period of sustained silence. It is important for the director not to prematurely assume that a final ending has been reached, because it often happens that after a short silence, some members of the group will start again and initiate new musical directions. These initiatives can be significant, and the director must allow for this. If the group has reached its own natural ending, and one person rebels against this closure, and tries to lead the group in a different direction, this may well represent a significant kind of resistance with important psychological implications.

When it is clear that the music improvisation has really ended, then the director and the full psychodrama group listen to a playback of the music. They should be asked, in advance of this playback, to think about some of the following considerations. However, it is critical not to mention these points *before* the improvisations, as this would create a level of self-consciousness about musical roles that would inhibit group spontaneity.

Some of the relevant kinds of questions to ask the group to consider, after listening to the playback, can include the following:

1. Who in the group initiated the music?
2. Who in the group was musically dominant?
3. Which group members were musically supportive of others?
4. Which, if any, group members seemed to be locked into their own musical expressions, without any connection to the group's overall musical direction?
5. Which group members appeared to be musically passive and unable to realize their own musical initiatives?
6. Did any members persistently resist against the overall character of the group music, rebelling and continually trying to lead the group in their own direction?
7. What lines of musical communication and rapport seem to have developed between specific group members?
8. What issues of symbolic musical transference may be evident?

Musical transference is a complex and interesting process. As an illustration, if a male figure attempts to musically dominate the group, is there a female in the group who resists this dominance in an aggressive way? If so, this could be an example of a transference issue, through which the woman is reacting against male dominance as a result of past experiences, rather than being a simple musical response without a broader contextual background.

Behavior that might be masked in ordinary social interactions may often be more openly expressed in this musical context. Such examples of transference reactions, when later discussed in the group, can lead to the identification of specific protagonist issues to be explored in a psychodramatic enactment.

As the group listens to the tape, identifying the group members by the distinctive sounds of their instruments, the ensuing discussion can raise issues that lead to protagonist selection.

If one person has clearly dominated the group musically, then that person can be asked *why* they felt so driven, and if that need to control was typical of their behavior in group situations, i.e., at home, at work, or elsewhere. If the answer is yes, a deeper discussion can lead to a reflection on the sources of the need to control, a possible related fear of loss of control, and so on. In this way, specific past or current issues related to controlling behavior and its effects on the individual and/or those around him or her can be identified. Subsequently, these issues can be used as a starting point for the ensuing psychodramatic enactment.

The same kinds of group processes leading to protagonist selection can develop from pursuing the other suggested questions. Lines of musical communication and rapport between particular group members, while excluding others, can have significance in relation to alliances and conflicts within the group that preceded the therapy session, and can be further explored.

If some group members maintained only their own musical expressions, disregarding the mood of the group, the issue becomes whether that is a characteristic kind of group insensitivity, and if that kind of insensitivity or rebellion represents a significant kind of general problem. Discussion of how these kinds of problems may have played themselves out in the individual's life can lead to the revelation of protagonist issues for psychodramatic exploration.

Regarding the individual who is unable to accept the group's musical closure, and keeps trying to prolong the music and initiate new directions, is reminiscent of the case of Paul, who was a participant in an extended workshop on musical psychodrama that I conducted some years ago in Paris.

In group work with Paul, his problems became more and more evident. It seemed difficult for him to keep in line with the consensus of musical feeling in group improvisations when the music would become subdued. He had been comfortable when the music was at a moderate or stronger energy level, but when the music became soft and introspective he was obviously ill at ease. He seemed to resist endings in music, the symbolism of which became quite clear later on.

Paul had been the dominant musical voice in a group improvisation. In the subsequent group discussion he dismissed any symbolic interpretations of his behavior, He claimed that it was the naturally dynamic and expressive qualities of the instrument he was playing, a melodica (a keyed wind instrument with a harmonica-like sound), that had been responsible for this, in contrast to the softer instruments of the others, and that it had not been his intention to assume a dominant role.

The following group improvisation was intended to involve the rest of the group members who had not had a chance to play in the previous experience. However, Paul was the only member of the previous group who insisted on involving himself once more. This time he chose a new instrument, a large drum, the single most powerful and dynamic instrument available.

In this group improvisation, he played the drum in an extremely dominant and aggressive manner. At this point it was no longer possible for Paul to rationalize his leading role in the group, and there was no mistaking the purposefulness of his expression. He was again insensitive to the overall subdued group feeling, and continually tried to move the group towards a stronger dynamic level. Paul would have been ready for a protagonist role, but time had expired for the morning session.

The afternoon session began with another collective group improvisation of all the participants and was intended more as a free emotional release for the group, a collective expression, rather than for any goals of group analysis. Paul again chose the large drum. This time, as if to symbolically express his frustration at not yet having been chosen as a protagonist, he simply would not accept the ending of the group improvisation, even though it had been quite extended with a good deal of energy. After everyone had stopped, Paul continued to play strongly on his drum, and tried to motivate the others to continue to play in the now otherwise silent room. His deep need to work out his problems was now too evident to be postponed any longer, and at that point he was moved into the role of protagonist. Paul began a verbal dialogue with the psychodramatist, in which he tried to explain why it had been so difficult for him to end the music and what the idea of an ending symbolized to him.

Paul expressed the idea that the musical endings were associated in his mind with the end of life and with fears related to his own death. This seemed to extend beyond just a general fear of death, but also involved a symbolic fear related to the many negative aspects of his family relationships, as well as his relationship with himself. This included a particular fear he had of ending up institutionalized in a psychiatric hospital as his sister had. All of this seemed to him to represent a kind of living death, which he felt summarized his life experience. In his attempt to avoid the musical endings, Paul tried to assert his great need to live, to express an affirmation of his more positive feelings as well as to avoid a confrontation with his deepest inner fears.

Because Paul had been frustrated in the previous improvisations by what were for him premature endings, and also because he had an apparent need to involve the group in an entirely different kind of musical energy, the musical director decided to give Paul musical control of the entire group. He was then able to use the group as his own instrument, to finally express through the group the great intensity of feeling he had been unable to realize in the previous improvisations.

When he was given the musical direction of the group, Paul was told that none of the participants (each of whom had a musical instrument) would be allowed to play until he would demonstrate for each of them, on their individual instruments, what their part should be. Paul went around the group and created a musical part for each member of the group. These parts were played continuously, and as each new member entered, the layers of sound were gradually increased, and built towards the final musical result that Paul had in mind. Paul seemed elated to finally be able to express himself in this way through the group, and predictably all the parts were on a high level of dynamic intensity, and with a strong rhythmic character. By the time all the parts had entered the music was extremely loud, rhythmic, and exciting, so much so that annoyed Parisian neigh-

Fig. 3. Musically supported soliloquy: "The group improvised a support-ive kind of sadness music to support Paul in the verbal expression of these feelings."

bors banged on the door of the therapy center to protest the noise! It seemed to create a cathartic and positive experience for Paul, and the group was totally involved in helping him to achieve this expression.

After he experienced this important release, I felt that it would be important for Paul to begin exploring the more introspective side of his feelings, his fears of death and general personal anxiety. He now resumed his dialogue with the psychodramatist, in a soliloquy, in which he began to discuss these issues as he walked in a circle enclosed by the group members, each of whom had a musical instrument. During this extended dialogue, the group improvised a supportive kind of sadness music to support Paul in the verbal expression of these feelings. This was a very powerful and important part of a whole week of psychodrama, and the music seemed to flow with complete freedom from the group that by now had experienced several days of work in group musical improvisation. What was particularly significant about the music was its total responsiveness to Paul, its sustained connection to him through sound, its every nuance an ongoing reaction to his words and feelings. This was a beautiful example of the continuous and audible empathy that can be realized through music from this kind of group support. Paul was able to verbalize these difficult feelings, while, at the same time, almost subliminally hearing and therefore feeling and benefiting from the ongoing group support that the music provided. There was a feeling of total concentration in the now darkened room and a sense of unity between Paul and the music and all the members of the group that is rare in any kind of group therapy. These moments were reminiscent of the kind of shared group involvement in the healing process that is more typical of the traditional shamanistic music and healing rituals in tribal societies (Eliade, 1974) than the more isolated and depersonalized healing traditions typical of Western culture, and the music sustained the mood which totally liberated Paul in his expression.

Paul's session later moved into a more traditional and nonmusical psychodramatic exploration of his general problems, but the music had served several important functions. It had provided an avenue for him to work into the protagonist role, and the sustained musical mood of sadness created by the group during his soliloquy gave him the emotional support he needed to begin to express and explore his deeper conflicts.

The group improvisation experience can also be used in other ways, besides its usefulness as a psychodrama warmup. It also has special value as a psychodynamic learning situation. For example, group participants who exhibit stereotyped and repetitive musical roles can make a conscious effort, on an ongoing basis, to practice taking different musical roles. This kind of musical behavioral change may initially be easier, and less threatening for many people, than trying to practice and learn these new social behaviors either in psychodramatic role-playing, or in real-life situations. This symbolic musical role-playing can enable the musically dominant person to learn to become a cooperating member of the group, or a previously musically passive person can learn to develop musical initiative and leadership. In this manner the musical group can become a stepping stone toward personal growth. This may follow a progression starting with behavioral change in the music group, followed by change in the context of psychodramatic role-playing, finally leading the protagonist to making substantive changes in the context of his or her real life.

Chapter 7

Music and Imagery in Psychodrama

You analyze people's dreams, I try to give people the courage to dream again.
—J. L. Moreno to Sigmund Freud

Guided Imagery and Music (GIM) is now a well-established and widely recognized music therapy approach that was originated by Helen Bonny (1973) and is defined as "a technique which involves listening to music in a relaxed state to elicit imagery, symbols and/or feelings for the purpose of creativity, therapeutic intervention, self-understanding and religious (spiritual) experience" (Bonny, 1977).

As discussed in chapter 11, music and imagery has a very ancient provenance in the practices of music and healing rituals in many cultures. While it is certainly possible to realize imagery work in a silent setting, without musical support, this feels inadequate if one has experienced both contexts. Silent imagery also seems to be in contradiction with the many long-existing practices of music and trance induction in traditional cultures around the world. When music support is provided, the music induces relaxation and introspection, and this in turn supports and sustains the imagery.

Music and imagery can be used effectively, not only by music therapists, but also by psychodramatists and other kinds of group therapists. While formal work in the Bonny Method of Guided Imagery and Music does require extensive and specialized training, this does not preclude the possibilities for otherwise qualified therapists, without this training, to generically draw upon the potentials inherent in music and imagery in an eclectic way and adapt some elements of this process into their work. These applications can be realized without necessarily adhering to all the strictures connected to the formalized Bonny Method, although those with a special interest in further exploring this area may be motivated to pursue a formal course of study through the Bonny Foundation. As will be demonstrated, music and imagery work can serve as an excellent warmup for psychodrama.

Music and imagery work generally requires a warmup of its own, beginning with a period of progressive relaxation. With closed eyes, and in a dimly lit room, the seated group members are gently directed towards focusing on slow breathing and the gradual release of muscular tension in the body. During this relaxation period, the therapist should explain to the group that they will be hearing some recorded background music shortly, and that during the music, the therapist may provide a verbal scenario to help focus the imagery, or that the therapist will be silent, letting the music be its own guide. The group members should be encouraged to keep their eyes closed during the music (as long as they are comfortable doing this) and asked to try to allow themselves to travel, as freely as possible, to wherever the music leads them. At the same time, the therapist should make it clear to the participants that there is nothing to fear, that they will always be in control, and that if for any reason they should feel too anxious they can immediately open their eyes and curtail the experience. Finally, the therapist should explain to the group that, after the music is finished, there will be an unhurried opportunity for each person to share their imagery with the therapist and the rest of the group. When the progressive relaxation period is concluded, and the group appears to be relaxed and receptive, the recorded background music is introduced. As for the choice of music, this is a significant consideration that will be dealt with later. However, in general, we are referring here to recorded instrumental classical music that is not too intrusive in character.

The content of the verbal suggestions, when recited during the music presentation is also very important, helping to provide a direction and focus to the imagery. An effective verbal scenario should begin at a neutral and nonthreatening place, serving as a kind of psychological baseline. This could be something in the line of "Imagine yourself in a beautiful, warm, green, and peaceful valley. The sun is shining, the birds are singing. It's a place where it feels good just to be alive."

This kind of introduction will allow most participants to comfortably enter into, and surrender themselves to, the imagery experience. Throughout the imagery process, the therapist's vocal delivery is also critical. The delivery should be relaxed, and at best, in a kind of synchrony with the music, a blending of words, ideas, and musical sounds.

The second stage of the verbal guidance will introduce the more projective aspects of this technique, in which the differences in the imagery experiences between individuals in the group will become more pronounced. Most people can comfortably enter the first, neutral, stage of the guided imagery, and most participants' experiences will be relatively similar to that point. However, it should be noted that occasionally some persons may not even be able to begin to relax, close their eyes, or believe in and enter a "safe" place that may never have been a part of their life experience. Others may be able to enter into this first stage, but be unable to go any further. Symbolically speaking, a metaphor such as a green valley represents the security of the known, and leaving that place and setting out on a path without a clear destination represents a letting-go of security, a kind of risk-taking that some participants may find too threatening.

The second and projective stage of the guided imagery should be more open ended, giving each person some projective choices. This could take the form of ideas such as a boat on a lake that travels to an unknown destination, a path in the woods that diverges in two different directions, or similar constructs. These suggestions are unstructured enough to allow each group member to have a unique personal experience that is generated more from within than dictated by an external framework. There can be some additional elements built into the verbal guidance, such as after taking the boat to an unknown destination to disembark and explore the environment, or to follow one of two divergent paths in the woods and meet a person at the end of the path, and so on. These give a little more structure to the guidance while providing some additional projective challenges. However, it is very important not to overload the verbal directions and devise scenarios that are too detailed, complicated, and directive, which would be certain to interfere with the spontaneity of the participants' imagery. In fact, the imagery scenarios should be as simple, clear and nondirective as possible, serving only to provide a stage upon which the participants can project their inner worlds.

The actual duration of the music and imagery experience is relative to the needs and experience of the group, as well as to the music being used, but ten to twenty minutes is a good general range. It should be noted that in the Bonny Method of music and imagery in group work, the verbal directions normally precede the music in a process of induction. The therapist is silent during the playing of the music and interacts with the participants again in the Postlude (Summer, 1998). By contrast, I have found the simultaneous integration of verbal guidance and music to be effective, which suggests that music and imagery is a rich area to explore and lends itself to many kinds of approaches.

SELECTING MUSIC FOR IMAGERY

The choice of music is an important consideration. While most therapists involved in this work make use of relatively calm, classical instrumental music, that obviously leaves the therapist with the task of trying to select from a repertory that encompasses an almost endless selection of works, many of which might be potentially effective. On the other hand, this musical variety allows for creative therapists to personally discover and make use of interesting pieces that seem to fit the needs of a particular group. However overwhelming the search for suitable music might seem, I believe that is still preferable to being limited by a predetermined list of recommendations. This could imply that other selections are not appropriate and inhibit the therapist's creativity in searching for new music and ideas.

The therapist should listen to as wide a variety of music as possible, listening for qualities that seem to be especially transporting, relaxing, or evocative in some way. This, in turn, can lead the creative therapist to think in terms of how a particular piece of music and a particular verbal scenario might best work together.

A well-known verbal scenario for imagery begins in a calm, green meadow, and then leads the participants to leave the valley and climb a great mountain. As the participants climb the mountain, the idea may be suggested that what is at the summit is unknown, but will be somehow personally significant for them. After a period of time at the summit, allowing the participants to reflect upon and absorb their experiences, the therapist then slowly guides the group back down the mountain to the valley from which the journey began.

In a generic way, an enormous selection of musical works could support this imagery experience. However, some specific pieces, more than others, might more directly mirror and support the drama of the journey with the changing character of the music. To support the scenario example just presented, I have often used the Andante movement of the Brahms Second Piano Concerto in B-flat Major, a movement that generally lasts about 15 minutes.

It opens in a tranquil way, with a very melodic cello solo with orchestra, perfectly supporting the image of a peaceful valley.

Fig. 4. "Imagine yourself in a beautiful green valley…"

At the first entrance of the piano, the music seems to take on a more ominous quality, and that is the point at which the therapist can introduce the idea of the mountain in the distance that may reveal something of importance at the summit.

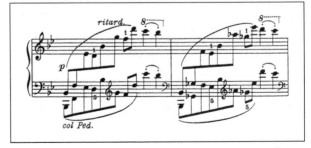

Fig. 5. "Off in the distance, you see a great mountain…"

As the piano part gradually builds in dramatic intensity, it blends perfectly with the imagery of gradually ascending higher and higher on the mountain.

Fig. 6. "Climbing higher and higher…"

After the music reaches its emotional climax, it becomes more subdued and can then reflect the imagery of the slow descent of the mountain. Finally, the same solo cello theme that opened the movement returns, and this is the perfect moment to suggest a return to the valley. This is a good example of how a specific piece of music can be selected to mirror and support the sequences contained in an imagery scenario.

In a similar manner, *The Enchanted Lake* by Anatol Liadov is an orchestral piece that has a mysterious, shimmering, and sustained quality that lends itself very well to imagery work. The intended program of the piece, that of a magical lake, works beautifully with a scenario that invites the participants to embark on a voyage on a magic boat, on a magic lake. A further suggestion might be that the boat has a will of its own, and that the participants should trust the boat and let it take them to where it wants to go.

Fig. 7. "Imagine yourself on a magic boat on a magic lake…"

These are just two examples that represent an effective union between selected music and imagery, in which the changing character of the music seems to parallel and reinforce the ongoing dramatic scenario. There are endless possibilities such as these for the creative therapist to explore. Through listening to and collecting interesting musical examples, and designing related verbal scenarios that work with the music, the therapist can gradually realize a collection of useful material for use in group therapy.

I have used a wide variety of music in imagery work, including such disparate examples as movements from *The Jungle* by Charles Koechlin, *The Swan of Tuonela* by Sibelius, excerpts from Bartók's *Music for Strings, Percussion and Celeste,* the Ninth Piano Sonata of Alexander Scriabin, jazz performances such as Miles Davis' *Blue in Green,* classical Indian music such as the slow alap sections from Ravi Shankar's recorded raga performances, and meditative pieces of Javanese gamelan music.

Each piece of music has a character of its own that can serve to elicit different feelings. Of course, it is well-accepted that all musical preferences and responses are entirely conditioned and subjective, and there is no way to categorically define the emotions expressed in any music. At the same time, in the broadest sense, regardless (or because of) the subjective reasons for this, some music tends to be perceived as calming for most people, in contrast to other music that most would perceive as stimulating. This does not suggest that there are any specific feelings inherent in any music, but rather that certain music elicits predictable, culturally conditioned responses for persons from the associated culture, even for musically naive listeners.

Even when a piece of music is generally recognized as conveying a particular kind of mood or emotional quality for most listeners within a particular cultural context, this does not assure that the music will therefore dictate the nature of the imagery. In general, a person's imagery experience has far more to do with his or her internal issues than it does with the specific musical stimulus. If a person is dealing with anxiety, anger, or depression, chances are good that almost any music suitable for imagery work could serve as a catalyst to help bring a person closer to confronting the feelings of these issues, although some music could be more or less effective. The music seems to break down the usual defenses, bypassing them through a right-brained and emotionally direct approach. Therefore, it is important for the therapist to recognize that a particular piece of music, in itself, cannot cause a person to feel anxious or sad or whatever. Rather, one can say that if a person was anxious or sad to begin with (whether consciously or unconsciously), that the music simply opened a path toward a deeper awareness of a preexisting feeling.

Another issue to consider is the previous familiarity or unfamiliarity of the musical examples to the group. If the music is familiar, it may then elicit very specific past associations for listeners, and this can be useful if the therapist is aware of these associations and uses them with intent in a prescriptive way. The only limiting factor here is that previous familiarity with music that is loaded with specific past associations will lead the imagery in a single direction, rather than into the kind of free and spontaneous imagery that is most usually desirable. For this reason, music that can be assumed to be unfamiliar to the group has the strong advantage of being an unconditioned stimulus, and therefore free of specific associations that could inhibit free imagery.

IMPROVISED MUSIC IN SUPPORT OF IMAGERY

Another area worth exploring is the use of live improvised music in support of music and imagery work. The music-makers can be drawn from the group, using the same kinds of percussion instruments that have been recommended in other group improvisation work. The special advantage of using improvised, rather than recorded, music in imagery is its flexibility. Recorded music is, inescapably, a fixed and inflexible entity with some inherent limitations, no matter how otherwise appropriate a recorded musical selection might be. If something becomes too uncomfortable for some group members during a music and imagery session, the character of the music cannot be changed once it has begun. In this instance, the therapist might be forced to choose between stopping the music abruptly, thereby disrupting the imagery experienced by the majority of the group, or allowing the music to continue even while it may be too difficult for some. Of course, the therapist could ask those having difficulties to open their eyes, while the rest of the group continues their experience, but this kind of abrupt interruption could create other difficulties of its own. It could well be better for those in some crisis if the music could continue, but change in a way that could sustain them, and if needed, guide them away from the area of conflict. Conversely, the therapist might also want to musically sustain an apparently positive experience.

When live improvised music is used, and particularly in conjunction with verbal guidance, the therapist can direct the character of the music, from moment to moment, to support the changing character of a flexible verbal scenario.

The musical group can create sounds that will fit with scenes like the peaceful valley, a boat in a storm, being lost in the jungle, or whatever else the therapist presents, with the therapist using hand signals to convey to the music-makers the raising and lowering of musical dynamics.

I have also worked occasionally with the Paiste Sound Creation Gongs in support of imagery work. This is a set of 11 gongs of various sizes and timbres, a unique group of instruments that lend themselves readily to support of imagery. Although gongs are percussion instruments, unlike other percussion instruments such as drums, which produce sounds that disintegrate quickly after they are struck, gongs are capable of naturally producing long and sustained sounds. If the therapist improvises on a set of gongs, the sustained quality of these sounds creates an almost legato effect, with the kind of sonorous continuity that helps to sustain fluid imagery experiences.

Because gong sounds are generally unfamiliar to most people, gong music is not laden with previous associations, and there are no expectations as to how they *should* sound. This tends to eliminate any participant judgments on the quality of the gong music being performed that could interfere with their imagery. Another positive attribute of gongs is that a single therapist may improvise both a flexible verbal scenario and the accompanying gong music at the same time. When the words and music are both under the control of one therapist, this can realize the closest possible match between these two modes of expression, the direction of which the single therapist can alter, as needed, throughout the imagery exercise. By being sensitive to nonverbal cues provided by group members, the therapist can, from moment to moment, improvise both words and music to meet the ongoing emotional needs of the participants.

The only potential disadvantage of using improvised music in imagery work is that it will inevitably be less perfect than any recorded music performance. This can sometimes lead group participants to judge the quality of the music negatively, and this factor could inhibit their involvement in the imagery. Although the instruments used in improvised music in support of imagery will often include instruments with relatively sustained sounds, e.g., metallophones and gongs, these still do not have the level of sustained sound quality that is characteristic of the strings that are so prominent in the recorded orchestral music typically used in imagery. Sustained and flowing musical sounds, without breaks, tend to be effective in sustaining altered states of consciousness.

In this regard, it is interesting to note that just as musically trained persons are often more inhibited in free musical improvisation techniques than musically naive persons, it also follows that musically educated people often have more problems in completely letting go and freely traveling with their musical imagery than do musically naive listeners. This is because musically erudite persons will often tend to relate to the music more analytically, such as focusing on the style, the composer, the performance, and so on, whereas the naive listener, unburdened by such musical knowledge, is more able to relate directly to the feeling content of the music.

In reference to the issue of past musical associations and their potential to elicit strong musical responses in imagery work, I recall a group in which I made use of the movement of the Brahms' Second Piano Concerto already referred to here. This was a music and imagery experience intended as a psychodrama warmup. As I was unaware of the group's background, I was unprepared for the strong emotional response to the music of one woman in the group. It turned out that she had previously been a professional cellist, and often played the solo part in orchestral performances of the Brahms concerto. Hearing the recording had been a very painful experience for her, which brought her to tears. For her, this opening theme was no peaceful valley. She was suffering from muscular dystrophy and could no longer play the cello. Music performance had been the focus of her life, and not being able to play was an unbearable situation for her. Her reactions led to a strong and useful psychodrama session, but the point to keep in mind is how familiar music may sometimes bring about unexpected personal memories for some, associations that may or may not be useful for a whole group process. For this reason, music that is likely to be unfamiliar is generally a better choice in support of music and imagery in group work.

Vocal music is also best avoided, since songs with words tend to be too explicit and directive and may hold the listener on a conscious level of attending to their meaning. Again, if a song is known to be familiar to an individual or to the group, and has specific associations that could be helpful in therapy, then this music could be used in a purposeful way. However, this could really be more a kind of associative music therapy rather than an imagery experience. Therefore, for most purposes, instrumental music is to be preferred.

Yet another possibility is using background music in imagery presented without verbal guidance. Music can be equally effective in stimulating imagery when presented in this way, and for some people even more so than when presented with concurrent verbal guidance.

The therapist should always be sensitive to the fact that verbal guidance in music and imagery may often trigger transference issues, and the gender of the therapist can play a significant role here. For example, if the therapist is a man and there is a woman in the group who has problems in dealing with male authority figures, past or present, she might react negatively to what feels like yet another directive male telling her what to do. This negative transference would then interfere with her imagery.

However, the negative transference, while inhibiting her imagery, could still have potential value in the broader therapeutic sense. That is, as in a projective test such as the Rorschach, virtually *any* response can be of potential significance and usefulness in the therapeutic process. If it happens that a group member, for any reason, expresses that he or she was negatively distracted by the therapist's voice, and that it interfered with their imagery, the therapist can still use this as an opener for further exploration. The therapist can ask *why* the therapist's voice distracted them, whether it was gender related, if it reminded them of a particular person, what feelings might be associated with that person, and so on. This disclosure, while distinct from an imagery experience, can still have the potential of opening up significant personal issues that can be used as the basis for psychodramatic enactment.

PROCESSING IN MUSIC AND IMAGERY

Perhaps the most challenging part of the music and imagery process for the therapist occurs when the music has concluded, and the time arrives for the processing of these experiences with the group. Initiating the music and imagery process is relatively simple, as it is the music that is the primary stimulus in eliciting the imagery, with the therapist's possible verbal guidance playing a secondary role. Because music and imagery is such a powerful method, it often stimulates strong emotional reactions in the participants, and the therapist must be prepared to deal with this material effectively.

Some group members might not immediately be ready to disclose and share their imagery with the therapist and the group, and this should be respected. However, to varying degrees, most members of the group will usually be able to share and discuss their experiences. The therapist must play a delicate role here. When engaging the participants, it is a challenge to ask only the kinds of nondirective questions that can assist individuals in a process of coming to better understand and interpret their own imagery, and without any pressures to follow a direction that the therapist feels is appropriate.

The kinds of questions that are generally most helpful here are "How did it feel?" or "What was it like when you were there?" or "Do you have any idea who the person was that you couldn't make out clearly?" These and similar questions are nondirective in an explicit sense, and they can help individuals to deepen their own self-understanding.

The following are some suggested guidelines for the presentation of music and imagery that may be helpful to those working with this process:

1. Make use of an introductory period of progressive relaxation before beginning the music and imagery session.
2. Choose an environment without distracting noises that can be at least partially darkened.
3. Use instrumental rather than vocal music, since vocal music is often specific in content and therefore too directive.
4. In general, sedative music is more likely to elicit and sustain introspection and imagery than stimulative music, especially music with a pronounced rhythmic character.
5. The character of the music should complement the character of your verbal scenarios.
6. Consider the advantages and disadvantages of using recorded versus live, improvised music as support for imagery.
7. Consider the possibilities of integrating more than one piece of recorded music or musical excerpts into a seamless whole, to provide contrasting music segments.
8. Think about music that you are familiar with, or may hear in the future, that you find evocative in some way. Consider its potential for use in imagery, and include it as a part of your own collection of music for use in imagery work.
9. Don't speak too fast when presenting the guided imagery.
10. Modulate the sound quality of your speaking voice appropriately.
11. Don't be overly directive.
12. Don't create scenarios that would be difficult or painful to imagine for certain participants, e.g., "Think back to the happiest moment of your childhood" for persons from abused backgrounds, and so on.

13. Leave time and space in your music and imagery presentations to allow group members to deeply feel and fully experience the music, and to explore their imagery.

14. Don't rush to interpret the described imagery, even if the symbolism may seem obvious to you as therapist. Rather, allow your clients adequate time, and try to guide them in ways that will enable each person to develop their own insights, and at their own pace.

15. Always remember that the biggest challenge in music and imagery work begins *after* the music presentation, and in the *processing* of the experience with the group.

16. Be sure to elicit responses from all of the group members, not only those who are the most forthcoming.

17. Try to develop participant responses and ideas arising from the imagery experiences, to develop symbolic connections, and to help the participants identify and better understand their feelings.

18. Respect ethical guidelines of confidentiality among group members and between therapist and participants.

19. Try to develop coping strategies for the participants, to help them better work with the problems they express.

20. Try to create lines of support within your therapy groups, helping individuals in the group to feel less alone in their problems.

21. Try to identify common themes or problem issues that develop out of a group experience.

22. Be open and nonjudgmental about feelings that may be expressed and shared, and be as supportive and helpful as possible.

23. Assure the group of the safety of the experience and of your presence as safeguard. Remind them that if the experience should prove too threatening, they are always in control, and can open their eyes at any time and stop the process.

24. Remind the participants that there will be opportunities for follow-up to their imagery experiences, and they will not be left to deal with any unresolved feelings alone.

25. If individuals in the group should express that they have had a particularly meaningful experience in music and imagery, yet feel unsettled in that they would need more time to fully explore this experience, remind them that they can always return to this place within themselves. Depending on the nature of the issue, they could either continue work with the therapist at a later time, using the same music to return to this inner place as a result of the now musically conditioned association, or if they are able, work alone with the music, in effect becoming their own music therapist.

Subsequently, the various issues shared by the individual group members can then lead to a profitable verbal group therapy session, from which a central theme may emerge, such as loneliness, fear, or relationship problems. The group discussion leads to further sharing and can be brought to some closure by discussing different kinds of coping skills in dealing with the problem areas being considered.

Taken this far, music and imagery work is a complete therapeutic method in itself. However, from my own perspective, having been involved in both music therapy and psychodrama, I have always felt the need to take music and imagery a step further, that is, to process the imagery experiences with the group through more than verbal dialogue, to move the imagery from the level of internal experience to the live and dynamic action of psychodramatic enactment.

MUSIC AND IMAGERY AS A PSYCHODRAMA WARMUP

The imagery experiences shared by participants in this work are often vivid and dramatic. They seem to demand to be taken into action, and therefore serve as excellent psychodramatic warmups.

My own procedure for making the transition between imagery and psychodrama is to determine whose imagery in the group seems to be the most promising for psychodramatic exploration. This also involves deciding if the person seems ready and able to serve as protagonist, if the theme of the imagery would raise issues that would be meaningful to the whole group, and just how much the person apparently needs to work on their issues at that moment.

Having made that determination, and selecting a potential protagonist, I will then ask the individual to close their eyes and to try to return to a critical moment in their imagery. As they do this, I will, at the same time, replay the same recorded music that was just used in their imagery experience. Since this music served as the catalyst in the first place, it is directly associated with the imagery and has become, in effect, a conditioned stimulus for reexperiencing the imagery.

I will ask the person, whose eyes remain closed, to describe, in as much detail as possible, the inner image before them of a pivotal moment in their experience. As this description ensues, I will silently direct different group members to take on the auxiliary roles of the people that are identified in the imagery and to take their appropriate places around the protagonist-to-be. It is important to arrange the auxiliaries around the individual as closely as possible to the described imagery. In this scene, the protagonist might describe something like the following, "I'm with my husband. He's sitting next to me on the grass. We're having a picnic. My daughter is some distance away from us, and she's crying about something. My sister-in-law has just come to meet us."

While this is being described, with the music still playing in the background, I would motion to a male auxiliary to sit next to her on the floor, then a woman auxiliary to sit at the far end of the stage area to play the daughter role, and another woman to play the sister-in-law. Then, when all the auxiliaries are in place I will stop the music, ask the protagonist to open her eyes, and tell her she is now *in* the imagery scene she just described. Her husband is seated next to her,

her daughter is now crying at a distance from her, and her sister-in-law can now enter the area and open the scene with lines such as the following:

> Hi ———! I've been looking forward to this picnic. How are you? And why is ——— crying? What's going on?

In this manner, a psychodrama has begun.

By beginning with a person's imagery, and then taking it into action, we can be confident that we are working with self-generated material that has real and deep psychological significance. Rather than being limited to verbal processing, psychodramatic enactment enables us to actively work with the imagery and bring it to life in the present as well as take it into the future.

In the imagery scene just described, the protagonist had felt that she was unable to comfort her crying daughter at the picnic because her husband and sister-in-law were so critical of her that she felt somehow paralyzed. This can be developed in the psychodrama. Going far beyond verbal description, in the psychodrama session she can realize what she hadn't been able to in the imagery. She could confront her husband and sister-in-law about their unfair judgments of her. She could act to comfort her daughter despite the negative attitudes of her husband and sister-in-law and further explore other conflicts that were implicit in the imagery. Additionally, once the psychodrama has begun, improvised music can be used to facilitate the session itself in the many different ways that are detailed in this book. In this manner, the psychodrama will have been musically generated by the music and imagery experience and then enhanced through the use of various improvisational music techniques.

The case of Victor was an interesting one that illustrates this process of moving from imagery to a psychodramatic enactment. Music and imagery can generate a direct and strong linkage to the psychodramatic experience and provide an invaluable and highly effective warmup.

Victor took part in a music and imagery session, and in the subsequent group sharing expressed that he had reached a point in his life where he was faced with two possible directions. He stopped and could not proceed, and at that point the imagery session had come to an end. Victor seemed frustrated by the unanswered questions implicit in his imagery, so I decided to use his experience to realize a transition into the protagonist role.

I asked him to lie down again, relax, close his eyes, and to try to fully recall his imagery of the scene at that symbolic point, using the same supportive recorded music that was used in his original experience. He described himself walking in peace and harmony with Gina on one side and Roberto on the other. I told him that when he opened his eyes both Gina and Roberto would be there. He could then take his imagery into reality and make the decision that seemed to be implied by the crossroads, the point at which the path divided into two directions.

Victor opened his eyes and found a "Gina" and a "Roberto" next to him, auxiliaries assigned by the director, and he was now living out his imagery in a psychodrama. He then embraced them and experienced a moment of a wished-for union among the three of them that could not exist in reality. In real life, Victor was stuck in a romantic triangle with his two lovers, and the choice between them went far beyond the specific personalities involved; it represented possible directions in his life as well as the ambivalence of his sexual identity.

In the ongoing session, Gina confronted him and expressed her inability to accept his relationship with Roberto. She insisted that he break up with Roberto. If he didn't, she would leave. Victor let her go, and in our later processing disclosed that this had, in fact, already occurred in his real life.

Chapter 8

Musical Psychodrama Techniques

MUSICAL ROLE REVERSAL

The technique of role reversal is fundamental to psychodrama, in which the protagonist takes on the role of a significant other in a relationship, and the other person assumes the role of the protagonist. Through this exchange of roles, both parties can begin to see each other as they are being seen, and as a result of this process realize new insights and learn to develop new styles of communication.

The process of role reversal is a strong and useful one, and it is used frequently in psychodrama work. When the protagonist is in dialogue with an auxiliary, and it is evident that the auxiliary is not getting the character and giving the protagonist the correct feedback, the director can ask the protagonist and auxiliary to reverse roles. Through this role reversal, the auxiliary can begin to pick up the essential cues that he or she needs in order to be more helpful for the protagonist. Role reversal is also valuable in helping the protagonist to extend beyond his or her own usual role boundaries and develop further understandings of the position and needs of the auxiliary character. Gaps of understanding between the protagonist and auxiliary can often be very great, and role reversal can provide a critical interpersonal bridge toward achieving better understanding.

As a way of introducing the concept of role reversal to workshop groups, and to dramatize just how disparate role perceptions can be, I have often used the example of the terrorist takeover that occurred some years ago on the *Achille Lauro*. In that incident, a group of Palestinian terrorists took over the Italian ship in the Mediterranean, while it was in the middle of a holiday cruise that included many Americans and other international passengers.

On board was a recently retired couple from New York, a Mr. and Mrs. Klinghoffer. Mr. Klinghoffer was not well and was wheelchair-bound. In trying to press their demands for the release of Palestinian prisoners in Israel, the terrorists began to kill cruise passengers, and their victim happened to be Mr. Klinghoffer, who was shot and thrown overboard.

Of course, Mr. Klinghoffer was an entirely innocent victim in this. The terrorist involved in his murder certainly had no personal grievance with Mr. Klinghoffer, and he probably saw Mr. Klinghoffer's death as a justifiable political action in the service of a greater cause.

For the role reversal exercise, I ask for one volunteer to play the role of the just-bereaved Mrs. Klinghoffer and another to play the now-captured terrorist. Led into a face-to-face confrontation in an on-board legal proceeding, how can they communicate?

For Mrs. Klinghoffer, her pain and loss are overwhelming, and she understandably recognizes no possible justification for this ruthless killing of her husband. By contrast, the Palestinian terrorist feels no reason for remorse, viewing his action as an act of faith and commitment to his people for which Mr. Klinghoffer simply served as a needed political pawn.

No two points of view could be further apart, and I encourage the two to angrily confront each other, and then to reverse roles. Such extreme differences in role positions makes good practice in learning to change identity quickly and to develop spontaneity—and also serves to warm up the group. Interestingly, long after I had been using this example as a warmup, the drama of this confrontation proved to be so compelling that an opera was composed and performed based on this incident, *The Death of Klinghoffer* by John Adams.

Similar role disparities can be found in a psychodramatic confrontation and role reversal between a Nazi camp guard and a Jewish prisoner, a Serbian soldier and an Albanian villager in Kosovo, and so on. In South Africa in 1983, when apartheid was still in full effect, I conducted a session in which one person played the role of then-President Botha, and the other his black African house servant, and the role reversal was very powerful.

When working with role reversal in an ongoing psychodrama, it may often happen that the protagonist will have difficulties in fully assuming the role of the other character. Perhaps the other's frame of reference is beyond their understanding, or it could be that the protagonist is inhibited in expressing a full presentation of cruel or insensitive behavior. To assist in this, the director ordinarily provides verbal doubles. However, music can provide another and highly effective way to help facilitate successful role reversal.

Musical role reversal may also be appropriate when the protagonist-auxiliary interaction becomes too wordy and removed from the core feelings involved. This process can begin by asking both parties to stop verbalizing and to each choose a musical instrument on which to express themselves. Then the director asks the protagonist and the auxiliary to continue the dialogue, only now through music expression and without words. As the encounter heats up, the director calls for continuing role reversals, even the exchanging of instruments associated with each role. The advantage inherent in musical role reversal is that the music improvisation tends to require a more clear and simple projection than most verbal expression, and it encourages both the protagonist and the auxiliary to get to the real point. The goal here is to encourage a more focused and less intellectualized kind of role exchange through music, and also to warm up the protagonist toward a more direct expression in a later return to verbal role reversal.

The protagonist may feel less inhibited in expressing different feelings in the symbolic musical language, rather than through the explicit language of words. Also, protagonists may gain a new confidence in projecting the *other's* behavior in role reversal through musical means, if that behavior has perhaps been too aggressive or otherwise difficult for the protagonist to portray on the more objective level of verbal expression. This can also be very helpful in assisting the protagonist in developing new insights within relationships. Finally, in musical role reversal, the symbolic expression through music can be the transitional stage in subsequently moving towards a more liberated verbal role reversal experience.

The instruments used in musical role reversal and other musical psychodrama techniques are drawn from the same kinds of percussion and percussion-related instruments used in general improvisation work. In musical role reversal, a shared drum is particularly effective. With the protagonist and the auxiliary seated on either side of the drum, the confrontation is very direct. At the director's cue to reverse roles, protagonist and auxiliary leave their seats and sit on the opposite side of the drum. Sharing the same drum is an intimate situation. The antagonist can physically invade the protagonist's space on the drum, which can be very provocative, and this readily lends itself to dramatizing role behaviors and stimulating strong reactions.

MUSICAL DIALOGUE

Musical dialogue has many of the same possibilities inherent in musical role reversal. When dialogue between protagonist and any auxiliary figure seems to be flat and overly verbal, missing the heart of the situation, or simply becomes unproductive for any reason, the director can ask the protagonist to choose an instrument and express himself or herself only through this medium. This could be a one-way music expression, with the protagonist communicating musically and the auxiliary responding verbally, or it could be a two-way musical dialogue.

In yet another application, the protagonist can be asked to make a single musical statement to the auxiliary, and then follow it directly with a verbal statement (see fig. 8).

In each of these approaches, the intention is the same: Musical expression on the simple instruments provided will tend to eliminate overly intellectualized interaction and encourage the protagonist to communicate feelings in a more uncluttered way. At the same time, the musical expression may well serve to fur-

Fig. 8. Musical dialogue: "The protagonist can be asked to make a single musical statement to the auxiliary."

ther warm up the protagonist to a different level of verbal expression, allowing the protagonist to, in effect, create his or her own musical double.

In many sessions I have found that by asking a protagonist to stop talking in the middle of an unproductive dialogue, to select an instrument and make a musical statement to a silent auxiliary and then return to verbal interaction, that the quality of the subsequent dialogue was positively transformed. The switch to musical expression often seems to trigger a deeper level of communication and helps to realize more profound connections. Musical dialogue is also very useful for a protagonist who is nonverbal, either generally as a result of some emotional trauma or with an individual who is temporarily unable to verbalize about a particular situation.

MUSICAL CLOSURES

In psychodrama, as in life, it may become necessary for the protagonist to bring closure to various kinds of relationships. This could involve situations such as saying good-bye to an auxiliary playing the role of a significant other in a relationship that needs to end, accepting the loss of a deceased person, or giving up a part of oneself and taking the often-difficult psychodramatic step of putting these things squarely in the past. Such endings may require much courage from the protagonist, to begin to truly let go in the symbolic encounter. At such sensitive moments, psychodrama directors often suggest to protagonists the possibility of bringing closure to a relationship without the use of words. This can be realized by facial expression, touch, a hug, or even by escorting the auxiliary off the stage area and out of the protagonist's life. It is not at all necessary for these closures to be realized at the verbal level, and at such moments, it is often helpful to allow protagonists to maintain the privacy of their thoughts and feelings.

Musical closures can also realize this advantage of nonverbal expression, which can protect the protagonist's emotional privacy. The protagonist can make these final statements to an auxiliary figure with musical instruments. Musical statements of good-bye are often very poignant, and when the last notes of a musical statement of closure are played, and then fade into silence, it often feels like the conclusion of a profound and composed musical work that truly symbolizes the final ending of a relationship.

MUSIC AND THE DIVIDED SELF

Music can be one of the most effective devices for dramatizing inner polarities, the dynamics of the divided self. So many life situations involve choices, such as to continue or end a relationship, to accept a new job or hold on to the present one, to take a risk or maintain security, to overeat or diet, to function in life as a child or an adult, and so on. Having to make such decisions is undoubtedly a normal part of life. However, we occasionally get stuck in the middle of these conflicting situations, locked into ambivalence, and sometimes for prolonged periods are unable to decide in which way to move.

When these kinds of inner conflicts become paralyzing, people often believe that these problems are a result of external circumstances. In fact, when the ambivalence is extreme, most such paralyses are more a result of internal rather than external polarities. The external issues may be real ones. However, they have probably evolved to an extreme level as a result of a person's inner divisions, reflecting long-established patterns of ambivalent life postures. A great advantage of psychodrama in dealing with these kinds of problems, in comparison with the more usual verbal insight-based therapies, is that psychodrama encourages us to go beyond introspection and to involve ourselves in direct and active confrontation with the issues.

Musical psychodrama provides a wonderful way of further dramatizing inner divisions and encouraging the protagonist to move towards definitive decision-making. After the divisions within the protagonist and the related issues have been clearly identified in a session, I will ask the protagonist to choose two (or more) auxiliaries from the group to represent the conflicting sides of his or her ambivalence. Then the protagonist is encouraged to dialogue and reverse roles with the auxiliaries, so that the dynamics of these polarized relationships become clear. At the same time, I will ask the protagonist to reflect on the feelings that he or she experiences when relating to the auxiliaries, who symbolize the different sides of themselves.

It may happen that the protagonist might feel that one relationship in their life feels passionate and exciting, while another is secure but unstimulating. I then ask the protagonist to reflect on what the feelings of either relationship might sound like if expressed through music. At that point, I will usually assign several additional co-auxiliaries to surround each of the principal auxiliaries to serve as music-makers to amplify their roles. The protagonist might suggest that the music of the passionate relationship be loud and vibrant, while the music of the other side flat and uninspired. However, the emphasis here is on *creating* the music, not just talking about it.

The protagonist might be asked to first approach the passionate relationship auxiliary group and to select from the available musical instruments those that he or she feels would best express the feelings of that relationship. Then the protagonist is challenged to actually "compose" the music by starting with one instrument, modeling a musical pattern on that instrument, and then passing it to one of the auxiliaries, who should then continue to repeat the musical pattern as closely as possible. The protagonist can then listen and see if the music sounds "right," and possibly model musical changes as needed. The music could be complete with just a single instrument, but often the protagonist will want to combine several sounds together. While the first musical auxiliary continues to repeat the modeled musical pattern (which would probably be loud and exciting for the passionate relationship), the protagonist can then add, one at a time, other musical lines played by the co-auxiliaries, layers of sound that build one upon the other. Finally, with all these musical elements now being performed simultaneously, the protagonist can make any final adjustments to assure that the music truly reflects the character of the relationship.

In the next step, the protagonist could move to the auxiliaries of the stagnant relationship, who should be positioned on the stage opposite the first auxiliary group. Again, the protagonist should repeat the same process, creating layer by layer the music of the flat relationship, which will probably sound weak, soft, and without energy or inspiration. While the music of this second auxiliary group is being created, the first group should be playing its music continuously. Finally, when the two musics reflecting both sides of the relationship have been completed to the satisfaction of the protagonist, and are now being heard at the same time, the atmosphere in the session becomes charged and imbued with a new energy.

The protagonist can then be placed in the middle of the stage. Both seeing and hearing his or her polarities emanating from the sides of the stage, the

Fig. 9. Music and the divided self: "Both seeing and hearing his or her polarities emanating from the sides of the stage, the protagonist's inner divisions are now exaggerated and blown up into a powerful symbolic form."

protagonist's inner divisions are now exaggerated and blown up into a powerful symbolic form. Then I often ask the primary auxiliaries in both groups to also take on a verbal role and to try to entice the protagonist to enter their worlds. The principal auxiliary of the passionate relationship group, while accompanied by the energetic supporting music performed by the co-auxiliaries, can summon the protagonist with statements such as, "Why don't you come over here? Don't you want passion and excitement in your life? How can you settle for a lifetime of boredom when life could be so rich, marvelous, and dynamic? Come over here now!"

While this is happening on one side, the auxiliary representative of the other relationship, while accompanied by that side's introverted music, can also call out to the protagonist, "Are you crazy? What's wrong with you? What are you doing now? You should be over here. Life might not be so exciting here, but at least it's comfortable, secure, and predictable. Are you going to throw it all away for a crazy moment of excitement? Come back over here!"

Typically, I will then put the protagonist at center stage in the middle of this dynamic musical confrontation, ask them to close their eyes, turn them around a few times so they become a little disoriented, and then ask them to move in the direction of the relationship that seems to feel best. In my experience, the protagonist will often move decisively in one direction or another, thereby making a symbolic beginning towards a new life direction. Sometimes, too, the protagonist may choose to stay in the middle. This could mean an inability to change, or it could also represent a realistic assessment and recognition that the division can be an honest choice, not a condemnation, and that they can learn to fully accept this ambivalence rather than resisting it. Another possibility is to encourage the protagonist to directly approach the auxiliaries on both sides of the divided self, first making an improvised musical statement to each, followed by a verbal expression of their feelings.

The musical possibilities don't end here. At this point, if the protagonist has made a clear choice towards one direction, this choice can be further solidified by asking the protagonist to say good-bye to, and express some closure toward, the auxiliaries on the other side. This can be realized by using the technique of *musical closure* described earlier. Another way to end the scene is to suggest to the protagonist that even if they have clearly chosen one direction over another, it doesn't mean that the other side of themselves has now necessarily disappeared. It may be helpful to recognize that some difficult parts of the past may be sustained without seriously interfering with new beginnings, and this may be more realistic than a black versus white assessment.

This kind of acceptance of ambiguity, learning to live with and accept some degree of inner division can be musically realized in interesting ways. One approach might begin by having the protagonist stand on a chair, as a way of symbolically rising above the present, and taking a step into the future of the person that they are now becoming. I then call upon the music auxiliaries of the preferred group to surround the protagonist, in a circle, and begin to again play the music that has come to symbolize his or her future. However, I then call upon the music auxiliaries of the rejected side to also join the musical circle and work with the protagonist to help him or her compose a *new* music to represent the future. With help from the director, the protagonist can suggest changes in the music, such as emphasizing one part, modifying or softening another, or eliminating yet another, until a new and integrated music gradually emerges. This example would probably still involve placing a dynamic emphasis on the spirited music reflective of the choice of passion over the music of stagnation, but perhaps still nostalgically combined with some of the musical qualities of the past relationship, a realistic middle ground that can musically symbolize a joining of the best of two worlds. Related to this is the recognition of just how powerful a protagonist's symbolic improvised musical statements can become in the session. For example, a feeling of sadness or pain, as crystallized in a seemingly simple and softly repeated note on a tone bar, or a drum, can, in the context of the session, become infinitely expressive to both the protagonist and the group. One protagonist expressed an inner division between a hoped-for clarity in his life and a dark spot that obscured this vision. His feelings of pain about the dark spot were powerfully projected through his improvised expression that consisted of a haunting rasping sound made by scratching his fingernails on the skin of a tambourine. When appropriate, the therapist can use this to advantage, by playing back this musical expression for the protagonist, on the same instrument, and posing a question such as, "This is how you express your feelings about your life these days. It really sounds very sad. Is this the way you want your life to continue?"

MUSICAL MIRRORING

In general, mirroring in psychodrama is a very useful technique in which auxiliaries are called upon to mirror the protagonist's general behavior and interactive style within the session. This reflection can be helpful to protagonists, as they can, at the remove of some distance, see their own behavior as portrayed by others. Through mirroring, protagonists can be positively stimulated toward trying new approaches to life situations that could be more effective.

An alternative to the standard approach of mirroring in psychodrama is *musical mirroring*. In this technique, auxiliaries are called upon to mirror the protagonist's behavior and styles of interaction musically. If the protagonist has been weak and ineffectual in confronting a feared other in the sessions, then an auxiliary can choose an appropriate musical instrument and approach the auxiliary character without words, improvising musical statements that reflect the protagonist's weakness and timidity in that encounter. Conversely, the music can be loud and strident if that would reflect the protagonist's behavior, or anything in between the two extremes. A potential advantage of musical mirroring over verbal mirroring is that it portrays the protagonist's essential behavior without being mired in words. In observing the musical behavior of the mirroring auxil-iary, the protagonist can't be tempted to say "I didn't say that" or "I wouldn't use those words" and possibly avoid dealing with the overall emotional truth of the portrayal. The musical statements can more fundamentally reflect the emotional core of the protagonist's interactions and cannot be rejected so easily.

The musical portrayal of the protagonist's behavior has the further advan-tage of avoiding words and situations in which the content is so sensitive that verbal dialogue could be too painful for the protagonist. These are the kinds of moments in a psychodrama in which the director might, in any case, suggest a nonverbal kind of mirroring, through gesture and pantomime. Musical mirror-ing is a technique halfway between gesture and speech, more dynamic than pan-tomime and less explicit than speech. This technique has parallels in work with adults to some of the principles of the Nordoff-Robbins (1977) music therapy approach with children. In the work of Nordoff and Robbins, a fundamental idea is to try to musically match the child's behavior—to create and return a musical portrait of the child. This is a nonverbal means of communication that can attract and sustain a child's attention, and open new possibilities for establishing inter-personal awareness and communication. In a similar way, in applying the tech-nique of musical mirroring with adults in psychodrama, the musical improvisa-tions directly reflect the essential character of the protagonist's behavior, and may also open new lines of insight and direction.

Finally, musical mirroring can stimulate the protagonist's spontaneity, moving him or her towards adapting new and more creative interactive behaviors in the session. As they see their behaviors portrayed musically, through the auxil-iary mirrors, in ways that may be newly revealing, this can inspire the protagonist to adapt new behaviors. The protagonist is encouraged to respond to the musical mirroring by experimenting with new musical approaches within the relation-ships being explored. These new interactive behaviors on the musical level may serve as an intermediate stage, hopefully warming up the protagonist towards eventually making the transition to new kinds of verbal interactions.

MUSICAL MODELING

Modeling, as a psychodramatic technique, is a natural extension of mirror-ing. In modeling techniques, auxiliaries go beyond simply reflecting the protagonist's actions, and move to suggesting, through active demonstration, new ways for the protagonist to behave and interact. If the group feels that the pro-tagonist could benefit, in interaction with an auxiliary figure, by learning to be-come more assertive or sensitive or polite, or subtle, serious, or playful, then the director may call upon different auxiliaries to try to model these new behaviors for the protagonist's benefit. It is hoped that this positive kind of role modeling will stimulate the protagonist's spontaneity towards behavioral change.

Musical modeling enables auxiliaries to demonstrate these new behaviors and interactive approaches through improvisational statements. As in musical mirroring, the advantages here include the idea that the musical modeling can express the essential nature of a behavior, avoiding the ambiguities of verbal expression, as well as eliminating any pressure on the protagonist to listen to the auxiliaries verbalizing issues that might be highly sensitive. Again, as in musical mirroring, the protagonist is less likely to dismiss the musical modeling than he or she would the content of explicit verbal expression.

Inspired by these different musical models, these improvised musical expressions can warm up the protagonist to explore new musical expressions directed towards a critical auxiliary. In the session, when these new behaviors seem to be well-established at the musical level, the director may then encourage the protagonist to make the transition to more spontaneous verbal interactions.

MUSICAL DOUBLING

I have already described how improvised music, created by the psychodrama group members and cued by the director to support a verbal double, can serve to liberate protagonists in their expression. The director can cue the music group to function as an independent and collective musical double, without words, or as a means of further dramatizing the impact of a verbal double, thereby providing the protagonist with musical and verbal support stimuli at the same time.

However, the individual double's role can also be extended into a musical one, without the larger group music support. In this approach, when a double is selected to work with the protagonist, he or she can select a musical instrument and move with the protagonist around the stage. The double can musically reflect and comment upon the protagonist's behavior as literally as possible or perhaps in a teasing way. If there is need to direct the protagonist towards a strong expression, the musical double can serve as a guide or even bring humor to a situation that is unnecessarily morbid or self-pitying. The individual musical double, like the verbal double, can musically exaggerate a feeling to help liberate the protagonist towards a freer verbal expression or integrate music and words as a combined stimulus. Putting the individual double in control of both words and music at the same time has the advantage of creating a completely unified expression, thereby avoiding any conflict in approach between the verbal double and the character of the group music-making as guided by the psychodrama director. The only possible disadvantage of an independent musical double is that a single musical double, with probably only one instrument, cannot realize the powerful musical impact that can be readily realized with an entire group of improvising music-makers.

MUSICAL BREAK-IN AND BREAK-OUT TECHNIQUES

The break-in and break-out techniques in psychodrama are very strong and energizing approaches that, if used judiciously, can be effective at the right moments in a session. These may be indicated when the protagonist needs to make a first step, to break through barriers that may be holding him or her back in a life situation. In the break-in, the usual dynamics involve situations in which protagonists feel themselves excluded, as from a group to which they aspire to be accepted, a desired situation, with the person always feeling themselves on the outside, looking in. In the break-out, the situation is reversed. The protagonists may feel trapped in emotions such as depression or anger and need to find their way out of a paralyzing situation. In either case, the protagonist needs to find the initiative to break through the inner barriers that may be holding them back from either finding a way into a new situation or finding a way out of an old one.

The usual procedure is to surround the protagonist with a group of auxiliaries in a tight circle, with locked arms, symbolizing the inner barriers that are holding the protagonist back from realizing their goals. Then the protagonist must physically fight their way out of the circle. It is important that the auxiliary group should provide some resistance, not making it too easy, thereby requiring a substantial effort for the protagonist in order to be successful, although the successful end result should almost always be allowed to occur. Often, depending upon the protagonist's degree of ego strength, the group might verbally taunt the protagonist at the same time, saying things such as, "You'll *never* have what it takes to be accepted in graduate school!" or "You're *always* going to feel inferior to the rest of your family!" hopefully creating a dynamic impetus that will stimulate the protagonist's resistance and rebellion and encourage the protagonist to take action.

At the signal of the director, the protagonist begins to break through the circle, and at best will emerge energized and inspired by this symbolic move toward definitive action in the session. Of course, as with all psychodramatic techniques, it is hoped that protagonists will carry out and build upon these new resolutions in their real life situations.

Break-ins and break-outs can be enhanced musically and dramatically by providing some of the auxiliaries with musical instruments. Then, as the auxiliaries surround the protagonist in the circle, some may be playing loudly on drums

Fig. 10. Musical break-out technique

and other percussion instruments. Others may be calling out verbal exhortations to action, and still others focusing on holding the circle. These exciting musical dynamics can add to the dramatic atmosphere, and in conjunction with the auxiliaries' voices, create a supercharged moment that will often inspire protagonists to action.

MUSICAL EMPTY CHAIR AND MONODRAMA

An extension of the approach of musical dialogue can adapt the frequently used psychodramatic techniques of the empty chair and the monodrama. In the empty chair technique, the protagonist interacts with an imaginary auxiliary. This can be indicated when there are no auxiliaries who feel prepared to play the role in question, either through a lack of adequate background information or any other reason, or when the protagonist is unable to accept any of the available auxiliaries in the role. In this case, the protagonist can communicate directly to the imagined auxiliary in the empty chair and can also reverse roles with the symbolic auxiliary, thereby creating a monodrama. The monodrama can be particularly helpful in a situation in which the protagonist may need to interact in a highly sensitive relationship, as with a beloved person who is deceased and for whom they feel unable to accept any auxiliaries.

In the musical empty chair approach, the protagonist can choose an instrument and make musical instead of verbal statements to the auxiliary in the empty chair. In a similar manner, in a musical monodrama, the protagonist can reverse roles with the auxiliary in the empty chair. Through frequent musical role reversal, between the protagonist in-role and the protagonist responding in the role of auxiliary in the previously empty chair, the protagonist can engage in an ongoing monodramatic musical dialogue. This kind of musical exchange also allows the protagonist to externalize and symbolically express the most private and intimate feelings of a relationship in front of the group, yet without having to reveal any of its specific content. This can be psychologically revealing to the protagonist, the

Fig. 11. Musical empty chair

director, and the rest of the group. Further, these kinds of musical dialogues may also warm up the protagonist to a greater degree of readiness for introducing a subsequent verbal continuation of these interactions.

MUSIC IN SOCIODRAMA

The sociodrama, rather than being protagonist-centered, looks at broader social issues, such as race relations, political divisions, group divisions such as teachers versus students, the police in conflict with gang members, and so on. Musical techniques can be used effectively to psychodramatically enhance the sense of group identification for the group members on either side of an issue.

For instance, a group song can be selected, or created, for each side of a politically divided issue being explored. The "liberal" group might choose a rock song, substituting their own words, or create an original rap to express their view, and perform this in defiance of the "conservatives," who might adapt a patriotic melody, adding new lyrics to express their perspective. The director can separate each group for a few minutes and allow them to prepare their respective musics. Then, brought back together on the stage area, the conflicting groups can perform for each other, in a kind of musical confrontation, a musical contest of wills dramatizing their commitments to their causes.

This musical device can serve to maximize the onstage role identification of both groups, generally stimulate group energy and involvement, and further warm up all participants in the development of the sociodrama.

MUSICAL SHARING

Group sharing, at the close of a psychodramatic enactment, is often one of the most important parts of any session. This provides an opportunity for all members of the psychodrama group, including those who may not have taken an active role in the session through playing auxiliary or musical roles, to share in the ways that they have been able to identify with the protagonist's experience. It is critical in this sharing period that the group members not offer advice or criticism. Rather, this is a special opportunity for the individual group members to personally share how they have dealt with their own issues related to the protagonist's and coped with those problems in their own lives. As in any form of group therapy, this is invariably helpful, enabling the protagonist to realize that they are not alone in their problems and that others have dealt with and perhaps overcome similar obstacles.

An alternative to the usual verbal sharing closure technique is to allow for the possibility of *musical sharing*. In this case, any group members who feel an identification with the protagonist, but are not comfortable enough to verbally share their experiences, can instead improvise a final musical statement. This can be a special kind of highly personalized musical gift through which, nonverbally, some group members can musically express the deepest kinds of feelings of empathy and support directly to the protagonist while others share verbally.

Chapter 9

Musical Psychodrama Case Examples

ANNA AND MARIE: MAKING CHOICES

Anna, a protagonist, was torn between a relationship with her former husband that provided only limited satisfactions and her fear of letting go of that familiar relationship to explore new possibilities. Her musical improvisation warmup had revealed a motoric sense of urgency, and her verbally expressed need for change supported what had been implicit in the music expression.

Her characteristic ambivalence and flight from commitments were characterized by her beginning her session with leaving and getting on a train, an enactment given impetus by the group's improvised and motoric rhythmic music. One group member described Anna as "the lady with the suitcase," a woman always ready to leave.

Anna chose two auxiliaries: one to play the role of her ex-husband (a familiar if less than satisfying relationship) and another to collectively represent the men she had yet to meet (the unexplored possibilities). Her dialogue between these two auxiliaries expressed the polarities of her own internal ambivalence and began to get bogged down in words, a repetition of her life's reality that even she seemed to find tiresome. Therefore, the dynamics of her session were changed in ways that it was hoped would facilitate her ability to begin relating to her internal polarities on a deeper level than she was expressing verbally, toward reaching a level of intuitive and undisguised feelings.

Auxiliary groups were formed surrounding each of the two auxiliaries she had chosen, and each of these supportive auxiliaries had musical instruments. One group, guided by Anna's specific directions and musical modeling, began to create some music around the auxiliary representing her former husband, a music created by Anna that expressed her feelings about that relationship. It was a quiet music, introspective, and without much inspiration or energy.

Anna then helped the participants to create the music for the auxiliaries surrounding the man representing the unknown of future relationships. This music was dramatically different in character, and had a great deal of tension and intensity. The director then told Anna to stop verbalizing, to close her eyes, and to listen to the two now simultaneously played musics that symbolized her inner polarities. The two musics were played at opposite ends of the room and, with Anna standing in the room's center, she was told to concentrate on the feelings elicited by these two musics. With her eyes still closed, she was asked to move toward the music that most attracted her, or to stay where she was. Of course, Anna had essentially composed the music for both groups, and these musics graphically represented her feelings about both possible life directions. In this kind of situation, by giving the protagonist the responsibility of creating the character of the music, through their instruments the musical auxiliaries become an extension of the protagonist. Anna eventually moved in the direction of the old and familiar relationship, but, as in real life, she was still not very happy there. She had honestly followed her feelings in response to this special kind of emotionally polarized aural tracking.

In a final attempt to help her break out of her ambivalence, the participants creating the two polarized musics surrounded Anna in a circle of sound. The music of her past, and that of her unknown future, were joined in a cacophony of sound and verbal exhortations, and Anna was asked to fight her way out of the circle. The musical break-out technique was introduced to help Anna symbolically break her way out of the circle of ambivalence in her life. Anna did break out of the circle, and, at least for the moment, seemed more relaxed and less burdened. One cannot hope to resolve any protagonist's deep-seated issues of ambivalence in a single session, but Anna at least had the experience of encountering a dramatically amplified expression of her polarities—and the opportunity to feel the emotional impact of her options.

Another somewhat similar session occurred with Marie, a teacher who was in conflict over a romantic relationship that seemed to trigger her feelings of ambivalence. Although she had a conscious desire to love and be loved, and appreciated her lover's feelings for her, she had difficulty accepting her own reciprocal feelings of love. This ambivalence, the desire on the one hand to love and be loved, and at the same time the inability to accept love that is freely given became manifested in the session as states of being in either a symbolic heaven or hell.

In this session, the director urged Marie to face the two sides of her ambivalence and to try to make a commitment toward one direction or another. Marie chose two auxiliaries—an angel and a devil—who each represented the guardians of the heaven and hell of her ambivalence, and divided the group into members of their respective domains. She had separate dialogues with the angel and the devil, each of whom tried to persuade her of the advantages to be had in their domains. Each auxiliary was supported by the appropriate improvised music from their groups, which Marie had helped to create: the peaceful music of the angels and the erratic and conflict-filled music of the hell of ambivalence. Finally, both the angel and devil began to entice her at the same time while accompanied by their very different musics. The chaos of sound could not have more dramatically or forcefully represented, for Marie, the dynamics of her ambivalence. Marie finally made a choice to try to accept the peace of acceptance and love, and later expressed that the musical representation of her feelings had enhanced her awareness of the depth of her conflicts in this aspect of her life.

The psychodramas of both Anna and Marie were very representative examples of protagonists trapped in ambivalence, and just how effectively music and psychodrama can combine to dramatize inner divisions in ways that stimulate the protagonist to break through self-imposed barriers. Whether or not Anna was subsequently able to establish happier relationships, or Marie learned to accept the gift of love, through their psychodramas they at least experienced new possibilities that would hopefully lead them in more rewarding life directions.

REGINE AND BRIGITTE: TAKING A CHANCE ON LIFE

Regine warmed up to her protagonist role through a determined xylophone improvisation that seemed to signal a sense of clear direction and a need to work on some pressing issues. Regine was divided between relationship conflicts, in this instance between an ongoing marital relationship characterized by stability (although apparently lacking any sense of play and spontaneity) and another relationship (past, but still haunting her memories) that was rich in the playfulness and childlike joys she was now longing for. The relationship polarities in Regine's life reflected her own inner divisions, her responsible and stable side in conflict with her long-repressed need to express her sense of play and childlike spontaneity.

Because Regine appeared to be so solidly "grown up," I asked her to psychodramatically regress and to experience being born again. In this new birth, she was free to choose any set of parents and circumstances she wished. She chose two very loving parents who teased her and encouraged her sense of play, very much unlike her real parents who had imposed a very strong sense of a "proper upbringing." This rebirthing scene was supported by group improvised music of an exceptionally gentle tenderness that enhanced the wonder and poignancy of this special moment.

In an ensuing scene, as an older child, Regine was given a party by her parents. A group of children was invited, and in this happy situation Regine was doted on by all in a context in which laughter, fun, and play were taken for granted.

Regine relished every moment of this scene, and she played in a way we had not yet seen in her adult persona. However, I did not want her to remain too stimulated by a fantasy situation not available in her present real-life condition. Therefore, we broke into her child-world and told her to grow up again into her real world and make the adult decision: to continue in a life of stability without joy or to risk the unknown and the chance of finding a new relationship that might possibly provide the opportunity to express and enjoy her lost inner-child. Although Regine was a positively transformed person when playing herself as a happy child, she still chose, for the time being, to remain in her only partially satisfying real-life situation. However, in a very real sense, a protagonist's psychodrama only truly begins after the formal session is over, when he or she starts acting upon newly acquired insights concerning real-life roles that were internalized in the experience. Much that occurred in Regine's session was growing inside her in ways that would find active expression in a later enactment.

Brigitte was a young woman, in the same psychodrama group as Regine. Brigitte complained about her romantic relationship with a man she felt was unable to really communicate with her. She chose an auxiliary to play his role and, given the directions to set the scene, seated him on the floor in a depressed posture. In role, as determined through role-reversal with the protagonist, her lover, Domenico, was as passive and apathetic as she had portrayed him. However, when she began to speak to him in his auxiliary role, she did not communicate any better than he did, and the two seemed to support each other in a co-dependent role of apathy. As neither seemed able to change their style of interaction, I asked Brigitte to improvise her feelings toward Domenico on the xylophone as a substitute for her repetitive verbal expression. The hope was that her musical expression toward Domenico might reveal another dimension of feeling that would take the session in different and perhaps more productive directions. To help Brigitte overcome any possible inhibitions, she was musically supported by the group members on other instruments. The group was instructed to move with her musically, to remain entirely nondirective, and to reflect and support every nuance of her musically projected feelings.

In fact, Brigitte's xylophone improvisation toward Domenico became just another reflection of their real relationship, and her music seemed constrained and joyless. I asked her if, in the past, she had enjoyed any relationships with males in her life in which she felt that there was a sense of the vital and direct communication that she stated she wanted to have with Domenico, and she replied that she did have this kind of connectedness with her father.

For the next scene, Brigitte chose a father auxiliary, and in this enactment we saw a very different, far more alive and directly communicative Brigitte. We then utilized the mirroring technique, asking for members of the group to work with Brigitte in a return to her first scene with Domenico, with the intention of demonstrating for her how she interacted with him and to assist her in obtaining a more objective view of her flat and uninspired style. We also called back the father auxiliary, and let Brigitte see a mirror of the entirely different and dynamic interactive persona which she brought to that relationship.

This was followed by bringing Domenico back once again, and asking the group to now model alternative approach styles for Brigitte. Each of the volunteers modeled a variety of different, but always dynamic styles of approaching Domenico to stimulate Brigitte's spontaneity in finding some new ways for herself. The intent was not for her to necessarily imitate the models presented to her, but rather to stimulate her to try to communicate with Domenico in some way fundamentally different from her usual patterns. However, when she began to verbally interact with Domenico, she still repeated past behaviors, and obviously was not yet ready to change.

As it seemed the time to take an entirely different direction, I called on two very positive and lively male auxiliaries to court Brigitte and remove her from her narrow world with Domenico. These charming suitors introduced her to a new sense of life and invited her to go anywhere she liked. She chose to go to the horse races, and this was a scene of great fun and spontaneity that was further enlivened by providing her with an auxiliary horse on whose back she had a ride around the room!

In the midst of this happy scene, Domenico was called back, and he was not pleased to see Brigitte laughing and happy and flirtatiously cavorting with two men that he had never seen before, and he wanted her to return to their old ways together without making changes. Brigitte again tried to interact with Domenico. I hoped that she would now be able to carry over some of the energy and spontaneity from her experience at the horse races to make a difference in her way of dealing with him. To encourage change, she was asked to again play her feelings toward Domenico on the xylophone, and again she was provided with the group musical support. I also utilized the musical-mirroring technique, in which members of the group musically imitated her previous apathetic approach to Domenico, as well as moving on to the technique of musical modeling, to provide Brigitte with some other dynamic musical models as alternate examples of communication styles.

While Domenico provoked her with continuing complaints, this time her musical expression directed to him gradually built up in intensity to a powerful crescendo, and her resentment toward Domenico and her dissatisfactions in the relationship now began to come through strongly. Brigitte later said that in spite of her fun at her "day at the races" and all the she had experienced positively in that context, she still was not ready to end her relationship with Domenico, nor did she know what she could do to make it more satisfying. However, as with any psychodramatic protagonist, the changes within Brigitte were just beginning to ripen, and, as with Regine of the same group, were fully expressed later.

ST. PETER AT THE GATES OF HEAVEN

As the two protagonists, Brigitte and Regine, were dealing with somewhat similar issues I decided to give them both another opportunity for growth in the group, even though their formal sessions had ended. I wanted to take advantage of the inner growth and change that often takes place within the protagonist after the session is over, and after they begin to internalize their insights and reach for new levels of spontaneity. Some time after their original sessions, they returned, along with the rest of the group, to find this director standing on a chair in the role of St. Peter, surrounded by the dynamic and powerful drumming music of the celestial guardian angel auxiliaries at the gates of heaven. Standing before the gates, dramatically supported by the music, which wonderfully enhanced the energy of this scene, I imperiously summoned the two former protagonists, Regine and Brigitte, to stand before me in judgment of their lives: their time had come! This St. Peter did not judge them on issues of good or evil or right or wrong, but rather by the degree to which they had been true to themselves in their lives, in following their own bliss.

They were each given a choice: to either make an immediate change in their lives or be condemned to a special kind of death. This would not be a physical death, but far worse, a living hell of perpetual ambivalence. St. Peter gave each of them just five minutes to make some changes, with the freedom to call on former or new auxiliaries.

Called first, and with the threat of eternal ambivalence hanging over her head, Brigitte acted immediately and decisively. She called back Domenico, but this time she refused to get drawn into his complaining. Rather, she grabbed his hand, pulled him out of the house and took him to the horse races. She began to take active responsibility for the relationship, and promised St. Peter she would continue in this way if he would allow her a reprieve, which was granted.

Regine, who was next, called on an auxiliary to play her husband, and told him directly that though she was not quite ready to leave him, she had decided that she had to begin to live her life in a new way. She had finally come to terms with her own needs, which had to be met at any cost, and was not able to predict the ultimate effects on their relationship. This represented a new level of honesty and step forward in her relationship with her husband, and so she too was granted a reprieve by St. Peter.

Both Brigitte and Regine were dealing with similar issues that basically revolved around the challenge of being able to embrace life in the fullest sense. For Brigitte, this specifically concerned a choice of whether to hold on to a stultifying relationship or reach out to more vital opportunities, while for Regine it was a decision of whether to allow her most spontaneous self to flourish or allow it to wilt in a relationship that did not nourish her in essential ways. In the psychodramas of both protagonists, these polarities were starkly divided.

Of particular interest, in relation to the psychodramatic process, was how the psychodramas of both women continued to play themselves out within them well after their initial sessions were concluded. This points to the idea that the full impact of a psychodrama really begins after the dramatic enactment is concluded, and that perhaps the deepest function of psychodrama itself is to serve as a warmup to life. With Brigitte and Regine, while their initial psychodrama sessions were certainly dynamic and productive, the protagonists' were still left with unresolved issues. It was only in their postsession encounter with St. Peter that the real values of their psychodrama began to be realized. The progression from initial warmup to psychodramatic enactment and then closure is a reflection of a continuum that ultimately leads protagonists to alter their actions in real life. With St. Peter, Brigitte and Regine made some new symbolic choices that hopefully were the first steps in their taking advantage of their psychodramatic experiences to enrich their future lives.

STEFAN AND HIS WOMEN

After a music improvisation warmup, Stefan emerged as a protagonist. His session grew out of information he had shared with the group in connection with his visit to New York for an important professional conference. He was deeply committed to his work, and he was disappointed and frustrated with three women colleagues with whom he was travelling. He expressed his concern that, for those women, being in New York was more of a shopping spree than anything else, and they seemed to care little about the opportunities for professional growth that were being afforded by attending the conference.

In the first scene of his session, he selected auxiliaries to play the three women, whom he encountered in Central Park. While they chattered on about shopping and sight-seeing, his pain and frustration were seething and obvious. However, his dialogue with them, even with the help of a strong and assertive double, was extremely passive, and he was unable to verbalize his real feelings. We tried to have him create improvised musical statements to the three women, and his music mirrored the same passivity as his prior verbal expression. At the same time, he openly acknowledged to the group that his double's statements were entirely correct: he *was* frustrated and angry with the women, but he was some-how blocked from expressing this to them directly.

This scene was followed by a dialogue with the director, in which he began to express his sense of deep sadness regarding the poor level of communication he had realized with the significant women in his life in general, in the past as well as in the present. He recalled experiencing continuous conflicts with his mother, as a child and now as an adult, with his wife, who was now in the process of leaving him, as well as in the present situation with his women colleagues. As he began to talk about these painful issues, the group improvised a sensitive and supportive music. As this music entrained with his growing disclosure, the whole atmosphere of the enactment was transformed, and he gradually became able to disclose on far deeper levels.

I then asked Stefan to explore some of the issues he had in his relationship with his mother. First, Stefan was asked to regress to being a child, and he explored a scene with her in which he begged for a greater level of emotional support. Despite her insensitive rejection, and his barely concealed bitterness, he was unable to press his demands. In a subsequent scene, from a more recent encounter with his mother, he was asking her for money that he desperately needed to continue his studies. He was again met with icy indifference, and he was still entirely unable to assert his unmet needs. His passivity also remained unchanged in an enactment, with the auxiliary playing the role of the wife who was leaving him. From the scene in Central Park, to those with his mother and wife, the gaps between his very strong feelings and his extremely inhibited actions were only too evident.

In an attempt to find a new way of energizing his interactions with these women figures, I seated Stefan in front of a drum. I then asked him to reflect on the feelings of frustration and anger he had experienced in the four primary scenes of the session, i.e., with the women in the park, encountering his mother as child and adult, and then with his wife. I wanted him to use the drum as an intermediary object to warm up his verbal expression, and I musically modeled some assertive statements.

The overall goal of the session had become that of helping him to find a way, at least within the confines of the psychodrama, to become more assertive and direct in his interaction with the auxiliaries playing the roles of the most significant women in his life. Of course, the deeper goal, as in all psychodrama work, was that he would be able to take any newfound confidence gained from the session to apply in his real relationships.

We then brought back each of the women auxiliaries he had already confronted, to face them again in a musical reencounter. First we brought back the three women in the park. As they taunted him for being far too serious and asked him to join them in their shopping, a verbal double expressed his anger at their superficiality. At the same time the group of music-makers, guided by the psychodrama director, was creating a supportive improvised music of growing tension.

Finally, this potent combination of music and verbal support triggered a dramatic change in Stefan, and he began to pound on the drums with a sudden and startling intensity and power. This seemed to help him break through an internal barrier, and while still beating the drum, he cried out to the women auxiliaries, "I need to be heard! I need to be recognized! I need to be understood!"

As the music group continued in their supportive role, he subsequently reencountered the auxiliaries of his mother and wife, and repeated this process. First he warmed up his feelings on the drum, and then he seemed to open his heart with strongly assertive statements of his needs directly to these auxiliary characters. It was hard to reconcile this now-flushed and energetic man with the passive protagonist he had been up to that point. The musical outlet had been a wonderful vehicle for him to release his spontaneity, and it enabled him to find a new power of expression. In the later group sharing, he discussed how he felt that he had made a new beginning, and that he was hopeful he would be able to sustain this authority in his real-life relationships.

MARIA: THE RED ROSE OF ECUADOR

In a session I conducted in Buenos Aires, Argentina, the protagonist was Maria, a young woman from Ecuador who had been living in Argentina for just three months. She explained that it had been a major adjustment for her to leave her family and her culture in Ecuador, where she had enjoyed a much quieter way of life, and to try to adapt to the far faster pace of life in Buenos Aires. Improvised music on a rattle in her warmup had expressed both her discomfort at the hectic pace of life in the big city, as well as a kind of firm determination and resolve to somehow persist and make a positive adjustment.

Maria was a student of psychology and trying to complete her training at the university in Buenos Aires. With the support of quiet and supportive improvised music from the group, she spoke of her sense of being alone, of having to make her own decisions, without real friends, family, or love in her life, "without no nothing" as she expressed it. Maria spoke of how she missed the slower pace of life in Ecuador, where there was real time for people and for developing quality relationships. She spoke of endless working and confusion, and the hectic rhythm of Buenos Aires with people frantically running throughout the day.

I then asked Maria to choose some people to represent her family and friends from Ecuador, the support system she had left behind, and these auxiliaries formed a small group. Next, I asked her to create a group of people that represented Buenos Aires to her, the people she now worked and lived with.

Then, we had each of the people in the Buenos Aires auxiliary group (about five or six) take a musical instrument and form a small circle. Maria was asked to stand in the center of the circle, and the group created a very loud and chaotic music to symbolize for her the turmoil of her feelings about the city. She had to then physically fight her way out of the circle, a musical break-out, to dramatize the conflict for her, and to focus her awareness of her feelings of anger toward the big city. The small group was a clear and defined target toward which she could express herself.

After breaking out of the circle, I asked her to speak to the Buenos Aires auxiliaries, and to tell the city how she felt. Buenos Aires responded by reminding her what a busy city it was, and how it just didn't have the time to waste on little peasants from Ecuador, and Maria replied by telling Buenos Aires that it had too much anger and too much anxiety. We also had her reverse roles, to become Buenos Aires, and try to understand the city, which had its own problems. As Buenos Aires, she said, "We're the best!" and criticized new immigrants such as Maria for being too slow-paced for big-city life. At this point it was apparent that Maria had begun to integrate some sense of empathy for the city.

Then I asked her to choose another instrument on which she felt comfortable, and this time she chose a xylophone. On one side of her I placed the group of auxiliaries that represented her family and friends in Ecuador, and on the other the auxiliary group of Buenos Aires. Maria sat between the groups, with her xylophone, in the now-darkened room. I asked her first to face the Buenos Aires group, and play on the xylophone how she felt about them. Her music was strident, disconnected, and somehow angry and abrupt. She said she didn't like that "tune," and that it was a sad kind of music. I had her turn around and face the group from Ecuador and play her feelings toward them on the xylophone. This time the music was warm, sweet, and flowing, in extreme contrast to the music of moments before, and she expressed real pleasure in this music.

Next, I asked all the auxiliaries in the group from Buenos Aires and Ecuador to mix freely with each other, to take instruments, and prepare to musically support Maria in another xylophone improvisation. I told Maria to think about the woman she was going to become in the next couple of years. She was never going to lose the Ecuador part of herself, it would always sustain her, and she would also be able to take good things from Argentina as well. I asked her to create a music of her future, the Maria-to-be, that would integrate the best aspects of Ecuador and Argentina.

She played her xylophone, musically supported by the members of both groups, and this time her music seemed to be a real integration of both previous musics. It had some of the energy of Buenos Aires, while still retaining some of the flow and continuity of the earlier Ecuador improvisation.

I then had Maria stand on a chair and look down at both groups that represented the two sides of herself and say some closing words. She saw that they were now all a part of her, and she even said "thank you" to Argentina for helping her to become a broader person in spite of her difficulties. This musical improvisation had become a symbolic beginning for her of a new kind of personal integration and adjustment.

We then had a closing period of group sharing and identification, and several people in the group were also immigrants to Argentina from other South American countries who had gone through, or were still experiencing, some of the same kind of adjustment problems as Maria. The group support was very helpful, as Maria realized that she wasn't isolated in her problem and that she would continue to keep on growing in her own way. Finally, we closed the day with a group guided imagery and music session, with some quiet background music, in which all the group members were asked to close their eyes and image going from a protected valley to the challenge of climbing a great mountain to encounter a significant experience.

As a very brief part of the relaxation and warmup for the imagery, and before the music had even begun, I had asked everyone to image a red rose as an exercise in visualization. After the music and imagery session was over, and the group sharing and processing began, the participants in the group shared a variety of experiences. Maria's imagery was especially touching. She spoke of the difficulties she had encountered, the struggle in ascending the mountain, how she had somehow held on to the earlier image of the red rose, and the way in which the rose had sustained her on the challenging climb. The symbolism was both apt and beautiful. For her, the mountain had become Buenos Aires with all of its problems, and she called the red rose that sustained her the "Red Rose of Ecuador"—that special and precious part of her that she could never lose. Music, through improvisation and imagery experiences in psychodrama, helped her to integrate her past and her present, as well as supported her in making new inroads into her future.

Chapter 10

Musical Psychodrama Scenarios

The following 15 scenarios suggest approaches to initiate group work in music and psychodrama, as well as some opportunities for the further integration of art and movement expressions. These are intended as guidelines rather than rigid frameworks. It is hoped that creative therapists will adapt these, as needed, or use them as models for the creation of new approaches.

1. The Concerto Technique

   Adapted from Priestley (1985).
   - Ask a group member who has a life problem they are dealing with, which they are presently unable to speak about, to be a musical soloist, and to express their feelings about this problem through music improvisation.
   - The soloist is asked to choose an instrument (or instruments) that would best express their feelings about the problematic situation.
   - As in a classical concerto, the musical soloist is never alone, and is always supported by the orchestra.
   - The soloist is encouraged to express the full range of their feelings through group-supported musical expression. It is critical that the other music-makers keep their music completely subsidiary to the needs of the soloist, without introducing any music initiatives of their own.
   - As the soloist initiates or stops the music, the others in the group match this. If the soloist gets louder or softer, faster or slower, introduces different rhythmic patterns, and so on, the group tries to mirror this music as closely as possible for the full duration of the soloist's expression.
   - When this group-supported solo improvisation reaches its conclusion, the soloist should now be more prepared to verbalize about the problem and discuss the related issues with the director and the group. This material is then utilized as a basis for psychodramatic enactment.

Fig. 12. Concerto Technique: "The soloist is encouraged to express the full range of their feelings through group-supported musical expression."

I particularly remember working with this technique with a group of health professionals in a psychiatric hospital in Italy. One patient, a man in his forties who had been wandering in and out of my presentations, was using facial grimaces, clowning, and other inappropriate behaviors as a means of attracting attention to himself. That afternoon he approached a group of musical participants at a very sensitive moment in the middle of the concerto technique and astonished everyone as he adjusted his improvised music along with the other group members, in a perfect synchrony of support of the music expression of the soloist. He showed a level of dignity and sensitivity through the music that would have seemed impossible up to that moment, a beautiful example of how musical sensitivities and empathy can remain intact in an otherwise severely impaired person.

2. A Psychodrama of Dreams

- Ask the group members to think back to a dream they may have had recently, or in the past. This could be a dream that is recurring and seems to have special significance.
- Ask a volunteer to share the basic idea of their dream.
- If the director feels that this could be important material to work with, the individual is asked to lie down and close their eyes, and the room lights are dimmed.
- Ask the person to share, slowly and carefully, all the details they can recall about their dream.
- As the person recounts his or her dream, the director cues the music-makers to improvise music that reflects and supports the ongoing character of the described dream sequences. The music should help to subliminally support the dream recollection, a kind of shamanic inward travel to access unconscious material.
- While the musically supported dream description unfolds, as in work with music and imagery warmups, the director motions the auxiliaries in the

group to take their places around the protagonist to prepare to reenact the dream sequence.

- The director cues the music to stop, the individual is asked to open his or her eyes and enter the reality of the dream, and this becomes the basis for the psychodramatic enactment.

3. The Musical Circle

- Ask the members of the group to identify the four most significant people in their lives.
- Then select an individual to volunteer to choose four auxiliaries from the group to play the roles of these four persons.
- The four auxiliaries should surround the protagonist, in a circle at the four cardinal points.
- Ask the potential protagonist to select an instrument (or instruments) and to then directly improvise a musical statement to each of the four auxiliaries, trying to express, as honestly as possible, how they feel towards each of them.
- Following the music improvisations, which should begin to warm up the potential protagonist, ask the person to now make verbal statements to each of the four auxiliaries.
- The director discusses the issues expressed in these musical and verbal dialogues, and the resultant material becomes the basis for psychodramatic enactment.

4. Drum Dialogue

- Set up as large and resonant a drum as possible in the center of the psychodramatic staging area. Supply two sticks or mallets and place one on each side of the drum.
- Ask the potential protagonist to choose an auxiliary from the group to play the role of a person in their lives, past or present, with whom they are or have been in some conflict.
- Ask the person to describe, in as much detail as possible, the nature of the conflict and the typical behavior of the antagonist.
- Ask the person to describe a typical kind of scene in which this conflict usually plays itself out.
- Without words, the protagonist and auxiliary are asked to improvise on the shared drum and symbolically play out the dynamics of their relationship.
- The auxiliary should, as much as possible, try to musically exaggerate the characteristics of the role character's described behavior. If the character is described as aggressive and domineering, then the auxiliary should attempt to boldly invade the drum space of the potential protagonist. Or, if the character is weak, then the auxiliary's drumming should remain passive and unresponsive to the other's musical initiatives.

- The drumming should energize and warm up the protagonist, and the director can then begin to verbally dialogue with the protagonist about what is going on in this relationship, and this is then moved into active psychodrama work.

5. The Dance of Life

Note that this and the following scenario both integrate music, dance, and drama.

- Ask the group to reflect on the idea that if they were asked to create a dance that would reflect their life, what that dance expression might be like.
- Ask them to think about the kinds of feelings the dance would express. Would it be a happy or a sad dance, with lively or restrained movements?
- Ask them to think about the kind of music that would best accompany this dance of their life. Would it be loud and intense, or soft and introspective?
- Ask for a volunteer to try their dance. As the individual moves, the group of music-makers should improvise music that mirrors and supports the dancer's ongoing expression.
- When the dance is over, the director then asks the individual to verbally share the feelings expressed in the musically supported dance.
- The dance has become the warmup to verbal expression, and this material is utilized as the basis for psychodramatic exploration.

6. A Dance to the Spirit of Wisdom

- Set up a kind of altar or sanctuary for the all-knowing spirit of wisdom, using chairs or other available material.
- Have each group member approach the sanctuary and improvise a dance in homage to the spirit of wisdom.
- As each person dances, they are accompanied by the improvised music of the music-makers that mirrors and supports their dance movements.
- When they are ready, each person will direct a question about their lives, out loud, to the spirit of wisdom.
- When the question is verbalized, the dance and music come to a halt.
- The individuals then wait for the responses to their questions to come to them inwardly.
- Then each person shares their question, and the answers they received, with the director and the group.
- The individuals with the most significant issues brought up in this sharing move into the protagonist role and psychodramatic enactment.

7. The Musical Time Machine

- Ask for a volunteer from the group who would like to travel into their future. This can be a week or a year or ten years or fifty, whichever period they would like to explore.

- Ask the person to enter into the time machine (a cluster of auxiliaries), to close their eyes, and to imagine themselves being magically transported to the future.
- Ask the music-makers to create mysterious musical sounds to accompany the time travel.
- The individual is told that when the music stops (after an approximate five minutes), they will find themselves in their future.
- The musically supported time travel can warm up the protagonist to enter this new future-based role.
- As they assume the role of their future self, ask the protagonist to describe the situation, and this material becomes the basis for a psychodrama of the future.

8. Death and Reprieve

It has been observed that people will often only fully value their lives when they are close to death and faced with the sure knowledge of how little time is left to them.

- Ask a volunteer to act out their own dying. Tell the person that their time is now measured in hours, or a few days at best, as the result of an incurable illness.
- With dim lights, the dying volunteer feels this sense of imminent loss, while the music-makers create a soft, sad, and supportive dying music.
- The director then reminisces with the protagonist. With the soft music continuing, the protagonist looks back on his or her life, on what they had achieved, and also about their regrets—the things they feel most sad about having left undone.
- Suddenly the angel of death, played by an auxiliary chosen by the director, enters onstage, and offers the person a reprieve, a magical cure for the illness and a chance to return to full health and life.
- The entrance of the angel of death should be accompanied by surprisingly loud and ceremonious music from the music-makers that should shock the protagonist into full awareness of this sudden new development
- However, the angel of death is only making a very conditional offer, and the reprieve from death is entirely dependent upon the protagonist. That is, the reprieve will be granted only if the protagonist can demonstrate that they would take fuller advantage of their life if given a second chance, and would try to realize all the things about which they had previously expressed regrets.
- The protagonist is brought into active psychodramatic enactment, and is encouraged to realize those changes, to finish unfinished business and resolve outstanding life issues.

- If the protagonist is effective in realizing these changes, at the close of the session the angel of death auxiliary congratulates the protagonist, and the reprieve from death is now final and unconditional. If the protagonist is unable to make substantive changes, the angel of death may compromise. Since some effort was made in any case, the protagonist will be enabled to go on living, but will be sentenced to remain burdened with regrets and ambivalence until he or she finds the courage to make real changes in their life.

9. A Musical Rebirth

- Ask the group members how they would feel about having a second chance at life, to start their lives again, and to be reborn, perhaps reborn with the benefits of knowledge gained from their present life experience.
- Ask for a volunteer to be reborn. The director should dialogue with this person about what they would want to do differently this time around. Would they want a different set of parents? A different set of life circumstances? What changes would they like to make in this new life opportunity?
- The person to be reborn should curl up in the womb in fetal position surrounded and cradled by supportive auxiliaries, with closed eyes, regressing to this sweetest and most protected part of life experience.
- With dim lights, the music-makers improvise a tender and soft musical background.
- The music continues calmly for some minutes, and gradually, cued by the director, builds up in intensity towards the moment of rebirth. This should also signal and stimulate the baby into readiness to emerge from the womb.
- At a climactic musical moment, the baby struggles from the womb, assisted by the auxiliaries, and enters into a new life.
- The material in this new life becomes the basis for the psychodrama.

10. Art and Music

This and the following scenario integrate music, art, and drama.

- On a screen, project a slide of an evocative painting such as an abstract or expressionist work, perhaps something from Picasso, Miró, Pollock, de Chirico, Rousseau, Kahlo, or others.
- Have each member of the group come up and improvise some music in response to the feelings evoked in them in reaction to the projected art image.
- Then ask each improviser to verbalize the feelings expressed in their visually stimulated musical expressions.
- Work with the verbally expressed feelings that seem to have the most potential and use these as the basis for psychodramatic enactment.

11. Drawing Your Life

- While playing some supportive recorded background music (to be selected, as appropriate, by the director), the group members, supplied with paper and crayons, are each asked to draw a representation of their feelings about their lives.
- After all the drawings are completed, the music is stopped, and the group members' drawings are taped to the wall for all to see.
- Then have the group discuss each drawing anonymously, trying to intuit the feelings of each of the artistic expressions. Following this, each of the individual artists are asked to comment on the group's impressions of their work, and to clarify the feelings they were trying to express in their drawings.
- Explore the most significant issues verbally expressed about these musically inspired and personalized art expressions and develop these into psychodramatic enactment.

12. The Song of Life

- Ask the group members this question: If you were to write a song about the feelings of your life, what kind of song it would be?
- Ask them if it would be a happy or a sad song. Would it have words and melody, or would it be just a melody by itself?
- Ask for some volunteers to try to find the inner song within themselves, in the same way as many shamans believe they receive their sacred songs from within, as a gift from the spirits.
- Ask for a volunteer to come forward to help realize their inner song.
- The director helps the protagonist to begin creating their song, starting with either words or melody.
- The song can be supported eventually by the music-makers, using simple generalized accompaniments. This can be as basic as a simple rhythmic accompaniment on drums or other percussion, a repeated ostinato figure on a metallaphone, or any musical support that would give confidence to the protagonist-composer.
- The director assists the protagonist throughout in creating and then singing their song, accompanied by the music-makers' group.
- The director discusses the song with the protagonist, and the issues it raises, and this material becomes the basis for a psychodrama.
- Another variant here is to create "The Rap of Life." Instead of song, this would involve the creation of a rhythmic chant that would express the same kinds of issues. Rap, being halfway between speech and song—rhythmic but not melodic—can be a more comfortable mode of expression for participants who are self-conscious about singing.

13. Speechless

- Ask group members to consider what they would do if they were to lose all ability to speak, or to write, or even to communicate through gesture and pantomime, with the only remaining avenue of interpersonal communication available to them being musical improvisational expression.
- Ask a volunteer to experience this deprivation in communication outlets, having asked them to first pick out some auxiliaries in the group to play the roles of significant others in their lives.
- Then leave it to the individual to express anything they need to these auxiliaries, but only through musical means, without the use of speech, writing, or gesture.
- This may frustrate and warm up the protagonist to the need for verbal expression. At the right moment, as determined by the director, restore the protagonist's power of speech.
- Use the issues that emerge from this reenergized verbal expression as a basis for the ensuing psychodrama.

14. A Day in Court

- A volunteer from the group will have to go on trial for the quality of their life up to that point.
- The director becomes the judge auxiliary and the remainder of the group are the jury members, each of whom is given a musical instrument.
- The protagonist is instructed to choose a good auxiliary lawyer to serve in his or her defense, while the director chooses a lawyer for the prosecution.
- The judge then asks the protagonist to be honest and confess their crimes before the court. Since no person's life can have been perfect, without fault, everyone has some confessions to make.
- The protagonist can also choose some supportive auxiliaries to serve as good character witnesses, and the lawyer for the prosecution can call upon hostile auxiliary witnesses.
- As the trial develops, with the protagonist speaking in their own self-defense, and the dialogue develops between judge, lawyer, and witnesses, the jury provides ongoing musical commentary as with a Greek chorus.
- If the musical jury members feel that the protagonist and/or his defenders are making good points, the music should be strong and supportive, thereby encouraging the protagonist to continuing in this productive line. Conversely, if they feel the protagonist is not making a good showing, the music will become increasingly soft, and can even come to an end in the worst case. In this instance, it would be hoped that this would motivate the protagonist to be more effective and to try to gain this supportive music reinforcement through a kind of psychodramatic musical contingency.

- If the protagonist is able to successfully win their case, perhaps by having called upon important auxiliary figures to resolve the conflicts involved, the judge will grant the protagonist their freedom. If the protagonist fails at trial, the judge will condemn them to live with this continued guilt and ambivalence until they are ready to realize some changes in their life.

15. Integrating Arts

The following scenario integrates all of the creative arts, i.e., music, art, dance, and drama.

- Some recorded introspective music is played in the background, and the group members are asked to draw what they feel in response to the music.
- The drawings are taped to a wall, and are each discussed by the group in a nonjudgmental way.
- As each individual's drawing comes up for discussion, they are asked to clarify the feelings expressed and encouraged to some degree of disclosure about the issues implicit in their drawing.
- Those participants whose issues seem particularly urgent are prompted to explore further and to create a dance that further symbolizes the feelings in their drawing. The dance can be accompanied by the same music that supported the drawing, and has become associated with those feelings. To make a direct connection between the dance as a direct extension of the feelings expressed in the drawing, the individual is asked to dance while facing their drawing which should be displayed on a chair in the center of the stage area.
- In this sequence, we see how having initially expressed their issues through musically supported art, the individual has progressed to movement that is musically supported in conjunction with the visual stimulus of their own art production.
- This combination of music, art, and movement experience should warm up the subject to a high degree of spontaneity to enter into a psychodramatic enactment.

Chapter 11

Ancient Sources and Modern Applications:
The Creative Arts in Psychodrama

In considering the relationships between music and the other arts therapies in psychodrama, it is interesting to examine some of the sources of psychodrama in the world traditions of ritual healing.

In traditional healing practices, such as in shamanism or spirit possession, healing rituals frequently involve the integration of all the arts (Moreno, J. J., 1995a). Rarely, in these contexts, are the arts utilized in isolation, as in modern single-focus music therapy, art therapy, dance therapy, or psychodrama sessions. Rather, they are seamlessly integrated, as in a ceremony in which the same healer may sing and dance, while wearing a special costume or mask, all the while involved in a highly dramatic ritual. J. L. Moreno, through the creation of psychodrama, which has the potential of integrating all the arts, was both calling us back to the holistic power and roots of psychotherapy, as well as pushing us forward towards bringing those roots back to life in a shamanically inspired and holistic therapeutic method. Many of the basic elements of psychodrama can be compared to aspects of traditional healing practices. A reconsideration of some basic psychodramatic concepts, in comparison with analogous practices in the work of traditional healers, helps place these techniques in the context of a broader cultural and historical continuum.

WARMUP

The use of a warmup is critical in psychodrama. A warmup is a period of time in which the director precedes a psychodramatic enactment with group activities such as the "Magic Shop," an exercise in bargaining with the shop owner for receiving personal realizations such as peace, happiness, freedom from stress, and so on (Blatner, 1988). This and other warmup techniques serve as a means of initiating group dynamics and bonding, of identifying potential protagonists and issues within the group, and stimulating in-group energy and spontaneity. Without this essential warmup process, it is difficult to overcome possible group resistance and initiate a successful protagonist-centered psychodrama. In psychodrama, not only do potential protagonists need to be warmed up, but the other group members also need to be sufficiently engaged to prepare them to play auxiliary roles and be otherwise available to support the protagonist.

A certain level of warmup probably takes place in almost any form of group psychotherapy, if not formally. Even the most traditional therapist might begin a session by asking group members how they are, or how their weekend went, and other similar questions. These ritualized and essentially rhetorical questions, generally eliciting the expected platitudinal responses, have as their real purpose to serve as a brief warmup. In fact, such largely symbolic warmups are often not sufficient to bring a group to a real point of readiness for in-depth experiences, and continuing group resistance may create barriers that the therapist has to struggle to overcome. J. L. Moreno (1953) fully recognized the essential role of a real and formalized warmup period, and here he was intuitively operating on a level of authenticity that parallels and typifies the humanistic practices of most traditional healers.

In the Peruvian Amazon, traditional healers guide patients through visions that are stimulated by drinking an infusion made from boiling cuttings of the ayahuasca vine, a jungle hallucinogen. The ayahuasceros, the healers who use ayahuasca, always prepare their patients for this ceremony well in advance (Dobkin de Rios, 1984). A special diet may be prescribed for the patient for several weeks prior to the healing ceremony, as well as other behavioral strictures, such as sexual abstinence. These prescribed directives can serve to begin warming up the patient, in an anticipatory way, to the special significance of the healing event to come. When the patient finally arrives for the ceremony, there will be further warmup time. Before the patient drinks the ayahuasca, the ayahuascero will sing special medicine songs, known as icaros, that serve to summon the healing spirits. He may also blow a purifying tobacco smoke in each patient's face in the group, all the while lightly tapping the patient's bodies with a soft palm leaf rattle in rhythm to the songs. This serves as a continuation of a warmup that began long before the start of the ceremony and maximizes the patient's belief system in response to the ensuing ritual and individual and group psychological spontaneity.

In the Greek traditions of Anastenaria, devotees of St. Constantine and St. Helen of the Greek Orthodox Church demonstrate their faith and special relationship with the saints through participation in a ritual firewalking ceremony. For several days prior to the ritual, the Anastarides warm up to the event. Dancing for several hours a day, over a period of several days in the konaki temple, in homage to the icons of the saints, they are continuously supported by a special music repertoire. The music ensemble consists of drums, guida (the Greek bagpipes), the lyra (a bowed string instrument), and singing. Through this extended and musically supported warmup, the participants build up their belief system to the point that they are able to walk on the hot coals without pain or tissue damage.

Traditional healers, such as those in the Peruvian Amazon, or participants in rituals such as the Anastenaria in Greek Macedonia, recognize the need that J. L. Moreno (1964) formalized, a warmup to precede almost any action. This is particularly critical in group therapy, to maximize the group potential for spontaneity, creativity, and receptivity to the therapeutic experience. Warmups help to remove the group members from the constrictions of the here and now and assist in transporting them to a magic world of infinite possibilities.

POSSESSION

Psychodramatic role-playing may also be compared to practices of spirit possession in traditional cultures. In spirit possession rituals, an ordinary individual may be periodically possessed by a certain spirit with whom he or she may have a special relationship. Guided into a state of trance by the healer, usually through a process of musically supported induction, the medium then temporarily loses his or her former identity. The medium, for a period of time, becomes a living incarnation of the possessing spirit. At that point, other participants in the ritual can consult directly with the possessing spirit, through the medium. A description of two cases of umbanda healing in Brazil exemplify the full power of possession. A young woman who was possessed by a wise spirit counseled her own parents on how to treat her, and another possessed man told others in the group to advise his own medium not to drink so much in order to avoid destroying himself (Figge, 1989).

In a similar manner, in psychodrama, fully involved protagonists, as well as auxiliaries who may be serving as doubles or in other role functions, may be as deeply possessed in their roles as the mediums in possession rituals. Just as the mediums totally abandon their usual identities in the period of possession trance, the psychodramatic protagonists and auxiliaries also set aside their normal personas. Trance is a basic feature of possession rituals and is usually defined as an altered state of consciousness that conforms to a cultural model (Rouget, 1985). By that definition, protagonists and auxiliaries fully immersed in their roles are also probably in trance states, as they travel freely and far from their ordinary realities.

The Western opera, a form of musical theater, depends for its full impact, like any form of theater, upon the ability of the performers to totally identify with the characters they are playing. The performers need to be so possessed by their roles that the listeners are able to suspend disbelief, and be persuaded that the actor-singers they are seeing and hearing are really the living personifications of the operatic characters they are playing. In this regard it is interesting to consider the experience of an African man, from Benin, who attended an opera for the first time in Paris (Rouget, 1985). In his account of the experience, the African relates how, in his first reaction, he felt as if he was in the middle of a possession ceremony, such as those he had experienced in his own culture. The singers seemed to him as possessed by other roles as the mediums in vodun ceremonies. For that moment, Birgit Nilsson was no longer herself but had become Elektra, setting aside her normal personal identity.

As he pointed out, perhaps all theater can be seen as a form of possession, and in opera he saw an even closer parallel due to the role of music that supports what he saw as the states of possession trance of the singers. In psychodramatic enactment, a form of therapeutic theater, we can observe similar processes at work, (i.e., trance and possession). However, art forms such as opera or dramatic theater may be seen as audience directed, whereas both possession ceremonies and psychodrama are participant directed. J. L. Moreno seemed to have sensed the need for an inclusive therapy. Just as opera integrates music, occasionally dance, art through costume and sets, and a dramatic scenario, so does psychodrama have similar potentials. In psychodrama, as well as in traditional rituals, possession is an integral part of a healing process that helps to liberate both mediums and/or protagonists from psychological boundaries.

In fact, for the psychodramatic experience to be fully effective, the protagonist needs to substantially let go of his or her normal identity, as well as ties to the immediate surroundings of the therapy group. To the extent that a protagonist is self-conscious and inhibited in fully assuming a new role, this may limit the therapeutic possibilities. This duality of being divided between ordinary reality and psychodramatic reality at the same time can be counterproductive. However, most protagonists are able to achieve a full role identification. This separation from the usual self, from ordinary reality, even if temporary, can have real therapeutic value in and of itself. This distancing, through role-playing, can begin to reduce the pressure on protagonists who feel themselves as overly possessed by their problems. Psychodramatic role-playing can be the first step in liberation from a problem, and just as in traditional rituals, psychodramatic role possession can be very helpful.

The very fact that protagonists and auxiliaries in psychodrama often need to de-role after a session testifies to the degree to which they were possessed by their roles. In this process, the psychodramatic participants may take some time to consciously let go of their assumed rules in the session and reconnect with their normal identities. De-roling is important, so that the protagonist and others involved in the session don't carry over any elements of their possessed identities upon their return to ordinary nonpsychodramatic reality. This is a potential role confusion that further underlines the degree of the depth of psychodramatic role possession, and which must be carefully managed by the psychodrama director. In the powerful healing through role-playing that take place in psychodrama, the time-honored practices of possession are integrated into the world of Western psychotherapy.

THE POWER OF THE GODS

In J. L. Moreno's early and epic work, *The Words of the Father* (1941), his basic premise suggests that each of us is potentially godlike, to the degree to which we are creative in our own lives. This possibility of playing god is a creative opportunity that is provided through the psychodramatic experience. This can be a helpful transformation for some protagonists who may feel helpless and trapped by their life experiences and may gain a new level of autonomy through this role. In these kinds of situations, the director may encourage protagonists to play the role of god and thereby seize control of their lives.

As god, protagonists suddenly become all-powerful and have the possibility to immediately realize all of their aspirations. Subsequently, even after the session is over, having attained this power psychodramatically, protagonists may then gain in the courage to be more creative in managing their real lives and liberating themselves from self-destructive situations.

In musically induced and supported possession ceremonies, as in the Afro-Brazilian candomblé or umbanda, mediums not only play god, they are believed to have become gods in a literal sense (Figge, 1989). Through this experience, the mediums are validated and temporarily empowered far beyond the possibilities available to them in their normal lives. As in the psychodramatic experience, they too may carry this enhanced sense of self into their regular lives. In both psychodrama, and Afro-Brazilian possession ceremonies, playing god provides the possibility for our becoming more truly godlike and creative in the way we manage our lives.

ACTING OUT

In the Afro-Brazilian candomblé, adherents are believed to have a special and lifetime connection to one of a pantheon of spirit deities. This connection to a personal orixa, or spirit, is always to a spirit that reflects and thereby validates the individual's personality (Moreno, J. J., 1995b). An extraverted person might be connected to a dynamic spirit such as Shango, or an introverted person to Omolu, the spirit of healing. In this way, an extremely dominating person would have no need to feel guilt or responsibility for his or her character or personal style, since it is seen as inevitable. As an example, for those who are acknowledged as spiritual sons or daughters of Shango, their dominating personal style is seen as their destiny, and inevitable, and that therefore they couldn't be any other way. In possession ceremonies, when possessed by their familiar spirits, mediums can give vent to the full range of their personalities. They can release their most extreme tendencies, far beyond what would be permissible in real-life situations, and in a protected context that is free from any possibilities of censure or negative judgement.

In psychodramatic role-playing, as in possession ceremonies, protagonists are also free to act out all possible behaviors, without guilt, as the responsibility can be assigned to the character of the others whose role the protagonist has assumed. In the psychodramatic method, the protagonist can assume the role of persons in their lives towards whom they may harbor the greatest fear or hatred, people that may be normally unapproachable. In role reversal, by playing the roles of these feared or hated persons, the protagonist may exaggerate the worst characteristics of the other. By enabling protagonists to become those whom they fear or resent the most, they can realize a cathartic release through expressing the other's worst behaviors. At the same time, in the role of a sadistic other, the cruelty that is portrayed against the protagonist, or others, may also represent the aggression that the protagonist feels himself toward his tormentor. The psychodramatic enactment allows the protagonist to express unlimited aggression, yet without any feeling of guilt or fear of later condemnation from the group, because it is clear to all that he is playing the role of another. The aggression is assumed to be not his own (although this may not always be true), and the protagonist's actions are seen as only a mirror of the other's behavior.

DOUBLING

It is an interesting semantic connection that effective psychodramatic doubles who need to effectively suppress their own identities in order to truly feel and become as one with a protagonist may be judged as effective to the degree to which they are able to get "in the spirit" of protagonist's inner worlds. Just as the psychodramatic double may exhort a protagonist to express a repressed feeling, so do healers in work with patients possessed by demons. In Madagascar, the healers will press the patient in trance to identify the name of a harmful spirit so that the professional medium, the tromba healer, can then mobilize his own connections to helpful spirits to combat the patient's demons (Sharp, 1993).

Rouget (1985) referred to a case reported among the Tonga of Mozambique in which percussion music was played with increasing violence and intensity for the specific purpose of inducing a sick man to declare the name of the spirit possessing him. This case is reminiscent of a music and psychodrama session directed by the author (Moreno, J. J., 1980). In this session, the protagonist was a woman who was trying to identify the meaning of a pervasive feeling of anxiety that she experienced in response to improvised music created by members of the therapy group. The director then cued the supportive and primarily percussive music ensemble to increase dramatically in volume, tempo, and intensity to reach a very loud, fast and rhythmically driving level. It was only when the music had reached its dramatic climax that the protagonist let go of her resistance and cried out the name of her husband. The emotional intensity of the improvised music provided the primary stimulus for that critical inner confrontation, and she was now finally able to explore the previously masked problems in her marital relationship.

A comparison between these two incidents is telling. In the case of Tonga culture, spirit possession is seen as the cause of illness whereas in contemporary Western psychotherapy problems are often attributed to repressed unconscious feelings. However, in both instances percussion music of growing intensity served as a catalyst that broke down the patients' defenses and allowed for inner awareness, confrontation, and growth. In both cases music also served as a musical double, supporting the verbal doubling roles of the shaman and of the psychodrama director.

Another interesting parallel with psychodramatic doubling occurs in Ethiopia. Special personalized scrolls are prepared for patients by traditional healers, upon which are drawn healing images that correspond to the patient's symptoms. These scrolls are typically made of parchment skin, from a sheep, goat, or antelope, depending upon the patient's horoscope. Further, the length of skin is cut precisely to match the patient's height, and to become a mirror image (note here that mirroring is also a recognized psychodramatic technique), so that the patient can be protected from head to toe. In this way, the scroll serves as a double. The spirit of the animal that was sacrificed to produce the skin doubles for the patient, and can directly intercede for him in fighting against harmful possessing demons in the spirit world (Mercier, 1997).

ROLE REVERSAL

Early on in his work, J. L. Moreno recognized the fundamental power of role-reversal. This is the idea that to the extent to which we can fully feel, experience, and empathize with another person's reality, in attempting to inhabit that reality, we can begin to more fully understand and appreciate another's perspective. This can enable us to modify our behavior through recognizing the authenticity of a differing point of view. This essential psychodramatic tool, through which even polar opposites can learn to communicate, also has its analogies in traditional healing. In Madagascar, people are considered to be possessed by harmful spirits if they sustain seriously disturbed behaviors that prevent them from leading a normal life (Sharp, 1993). In the case of continuing problems of this kind, the sick individual, or those responsible for him, may often seek the help of the professional Malagasy mediums known as trombas, or ombiasi. In a musically induced trance, the tromba medium, with his connections to the spirits of deceased Malagasy royalty, can combat the destructive spirits to save the patient. In some sense, the possessed patient has reversed roles with the demonic possessing spirit. If the tromba healer is successful in exorcising the demonic spirit, the patient may be restored to his usual role. The patient, having symbolically experienced the pain of the demonic reality, may then become extra prudent in trying to avoid again breaking any of the many and highly restrictive fady, the Malagasy taboos. It is usually believed that having broken the rules of fady may have been what initially brought about the negative possession. This role reversal with the demonic spirit can have served a productive purpose if the patient is able to later return to his normal role identity.

Another example of role reversal can be seen in the remarkable birth dance, the Kapanga of western Kenya (Mulindi-King, 1990). In Kenya, this dance can only be performed by women who themselves have given birth, and it is performed for just one woman, who is in labor. When she begins to go into labor, she calls out, and all the women who have previously given birth in the village surround her house—no men may perform this dance. The women form a circle and perform a violently rhythmic dance with song that is punctuated by rhythmic clapping. Unlike other polyrhythmic African musics, the combined song, dance/movement, and clapping all share a single clear and fast rhythmic pattern—a pattern designed to match and entrain the rhythm of giving birth as the dance continues until the child is born. The words of the accompanying song speak of pain in the first person-"I have this pain, this awful pain" as the dancers identify with and reverse roles with the mother. This role reversal also takes on dimensions of doubling and mirroring, as the dancers psychologically incorporate the protagonist's pain.

All of this is done for the support of the birthing mother. Everything in this practice—the empathic words, the dance, and the clapping—all express a single rhythmic pattern. And this continues until the mother begins to breathe with the pulse and is assisted by midwives as she delivers her child. Finally, in this practice, as in many other traditional healing rituals, we see the power of group therapy that is also integral to the psychodramatic process.

DEATH AND REBIRTH

The name of the hallucinogenic vine used in Amazonian visionary healing, ayahuasca, is a Quechua Indian word that is usually translated as "vine of the soul" (Schultes and Raffouf, 1992). It is claimed that the power of the visionary experience is such that the soul leaves the body to directly encounter the spirit world (Trupp, 1981). Having symbolically come to the edge of death in this way, the patient is then able to return to life with new insights and appreciation.

There is also a parallel with the healing dances of the !Kung bushmen of Namibia and Botswana. The !Kung carry out all-night medicine dances in a state of deep trance, with the male healers dancing, while the women provide support through rhythmic clapping and song. At the height of their trance states, the men appear to be unconscious, in a state of "half-death" (Marshall, 1969). In their belief system, it is thought that the spirits have left their bodies in order to combat the spirits of illness that may be threatening the health of other members of the group. Through these near-death experiences, the healers can bring back knowledge and power to help those whom they are curing.

Similarly, in psychodrama, it is also possible to experience and learn from a symbolic death experience (Blatner, 1988). In part, death implies letting go, giving up the things that we most cherish in life. To experience and feel the full impact of these losses in a psychodramatic enactment, and then to be returned to life, enables the protagonist to have a renewed appreciation of things which may have previously been taken for granted. This can be an invaluable learning experience that can inspire the protagonist to live more fully in the present.

In psychodrama, as in traditional healing practices, the protagonist may also have a kind of dialogue with significant others who have died, through auxiliaries playing their roles. This dialogue can help the protagonist to resolve issues of unfinished business with those who are gone. Through their auxiliary representatives, the dead can symbolically provide counsel and comfort to the living and can assist the protagonist in coming to better terms with these kinds of unresolved issues. This psychodramatic experience is very reminiscent of the shamanic experience of contact with the souls of the dead, in which healers and patients can "receive their teaching: for the dead know everything" (Eliade, 1974). Experiencing and learning from one's symbolic death, or through auxiliary dialogue to have contact and support from those in the protagonist's life who are deceased, is yet another unique opportunity made available through the psychodramatic experience. Psychodrama makes this enriching shamanic adventure available to patients in the context of modern Western psychotherapy.

DIVINING THE FUTURE

Divination is a common element in many traditional healing practices. Typically, the diviner may randomly scatter such objects as bones and cowrie shells, and from their configuration read into the client's future. By comparison, in psychodrama, as in the future projection technique, rather than being bound to an inevitable and preordained fate revealed through prophesy, the psychodramatic protagonist can directly experience and weigh the comparative values of alternative futures, and all in the here and now of the psychodrama session (Blatner, 1988). In the enactment, the protagonists can learn from these experiences, and as a result, become more efficient in the present to help realize their optimum future destinies.

In this way, future projection is related to divination, but it enables protagonists to become their own diviners and empowers them to choose their own futures, rather than surrendering to a fate over which they have no control.

PSYCHODRAMA: A HOLISTIC METHOD

Improvised music can further enhance the dramatic and therapeutic effects of psychodrama. This was explored by J. L. Moreno (1964) in the 1930s and later developed by the author (Moreno, J. J., 1980, 1985, 1991). In musical psychodrama, musical warmups such as music and imagery and projective music improvisation are nothing less than musical forms of psychodramatic trance induction.

J. L. Moreno (1964) also collaborated with the pioneering dance therapist, Marion Chace, who introduced movement expression as a psychodramatic option (Chace, 1945). Other psychodramatists have since explored the use of archetypal masks in psychodrama, introducing the dimension of art (Bingham, 1970). Through these examples we see how psychodrama can be a fully integrated therapy that can contain all of the creative arts simultaneously—music, art, dance, and drama.

Every person has a preferred and most natural form of expression, whether it be verbal, musical, artistic, or physical movement, and most typically, through some combination of these elements. Psychodrama allows for any and all combinations of these forms of expression. Further, psychodrama is a fluid method that is continually evolving in the hands of creative practitioners. This properly reflects J. L. Moreno's (1964) own dictum, that the psychodramatic process, as with any creative product, should not be frozen in the image of its original conception. Rather, it should serve as a model to stimulate further creativity and growth.

There is another related issue, and that is the performance of healing. In order to be convincing and helpful to patients, whether in traditional practices or modern psychotherapy, the healer must be an effective performer. This goes beyond knowledge and expertise in a field, but is rather connected to the ability to bring that knowledge to life, to dramatize it in a way that fully involves the patient. No amount of knowledge or training can substitute for this ability. Kendall (1996) cites an interesting example of a Korean woman in apprentice training to be a traditional Korean shaman, a mudang. She had carefully studied and learned all the traditional Korean songs, dances, recitations, and other necessary material she needed to know in order to be a professional medium in the exorcistic Korean kut ceremonies. However, when the time came for her debut with clients, she was unable to convey the drama of her possession with any power or authority. She was "correct," but she could not inspire, and thus was unable to establish herself as an independent healer. J. L. Moreno (1964) has shown us the importance of bringing roles to life and the critical significance of the performance of healing.

In conclusion, it is evident that the psychodramatic concepts considered here, including warmup, acting out, doubling, role reversal, death and rebirth, group therapy, and exploring the future, all have clear connections to cultural and historical precedents. The psychodramatic method, created by J. L. Moreno can fully realize the dramatic power and holistic breadth of traditional healing rituals, providing a new stage for these rich practices in the context of modern Western psychotherapy.

Chapter 12

A Look to the Future

You are surrounded by adventure. You have no idea what is in store for you, but you will, if you are wise and know the art of travel, let yourself go on the stream of the unknown and accept whatever comes in the spirit in which the gods may offer it.

—Freya Stark,
Baghdad Sketches

If current trends are any indication of the future, in which the creative arts therapies are becoming increasingly recognized, then the future should realize an ever-closer union between allopathic medicine and the arts therapies in health care.

In that regard, we can also anticipate less strict separations in the education and clinical practice of creative arts therapists. However specialized the modalities of music, art, dance, and drama, their complementary affinities are evident and should be utilized to full advantage.

It is certainly possible to dance without music, or to experience imagery in silence, and so on, but why should we adhere to these kinds of boundaries? Does the fact that psychodrama *can* be effective without music, or that music therapy can be realized without the integration of expressive movement, or art, or psychodramatic techniques, mean that we must maintain these kinds of unnecessary divisions?

On the contrary, I believe that we should be working towards greater interdisciplinary cooperation. Some directions for the integration of music and psychodrama have been presented here, as well as for including elements of art and dance, but these are only a beginning. There is no reason why patients of the future should not have the opportunity to routinely participate in group therapy sessions in which music, art, dance, and psychodrama therapists will co-lead group work together, allowing participants the opportunities of making use of the greatest possible variety of expressive and therapeutic outlets.

The education of creative arts therapists also plays a critical role here. Certainly it requires an intense focusing on the primary skills and related therapy techniques in each of the creative arts therapies in order to realize professional competencies in these areas. However, to the extent that this focusing is so narrow that it excludes providing some basic grounding in the complementary arts disciplines, this may be working against the realization of future creative arts therapists who will have a more collaborative frame of reference.

One way to achieve this is to consider requiring some introductory coursework in the related arts therapies for students majoring in any of these disciplines. As an example, music therapy students could take introductory level courses in art therapy, dance therapy, and psychodrama, or psychodrama students could take introductory courses in music therapy, art therapy, dance therapy, and so on. If this should prove to be initially difficult, in terms of the pragmatics of available faculty, or the pressure of already heavy degree plans or other educational or training programs, then perhaps this could be initiated by inviting guest lecturers from the related disciplines to offer a number of required class hours in their respective topics. These might be offered within the framework of preexisting introductory classes in the primary discipline, at least providing a general orientation to the other arts therapies. This could be the beginning of helping students in the creative arts therapies to develop an interdisciplinary mindset and would be further enhanced by providing integrated experiences for these students in the settings of their supervised practicum hours in clinical sites. Interdisciplinary clinical experiences of this kind could involve collaborative work with students representing all of the creative arts therapies, providing the opportunity for hands-on training that would hopefully inspire the graduates of these programs to continue to develop these approaches in their eventual professional work.

During the Holocaust, in concentration camps such as Auschwitz, deprived of every vestige of dignity and in the most brutal circumstances of suffering and dehumanization, some prisoners still sought out music in the way of singing with and for each other, as a way of reaffirming their humanity and their will to survive (Moreno, J. J., 1999). Others, including children, left their art work on the barracks walls as their last expression.

Brian Keenan (1992), a long-term hostage in Beirut in the 1980s, was kept in extreme conditions of solitary confinement in a dark cell. At one point, near the brink of madness, he suddenly began to "hear" music, music that he clearly heard while knowing that it wasn't really there. Still, this imagined music was irresistible for him, and he heard all the music he remembered from his life experience. As Keenan expressed it (1992), "It seemed I sat alone in a great concert hall in which this music was being played for me alone. I heard the ethnic music of Africa. The rhythmic music of bone on skin. I heard the swirl and squeal of bagpipes. I heard voices chanting in a tribal chant; great orchestras of violins; and flutes filled the air like bird flight while quiet voices sang some ancient Gregorian chants. All the music of the world was there, playing incessantly into my cell." Carried away by this imagined music, he began to dance in a frenzy of exultation, and somehow, through this ecstatic and cathartic expression, he found the strength to hold on to his sanity and survive until his eventual release.

Such examples as these are testament to the fact that the expressive arts are far more than a luxury. They are, in fact, a necessity for the human spirit. People seek out these kinds of expression, to make music, to move, to create art, or to act out, even when these opportunities are not provided, and in the most deprived circumstances. There are no divisions to human expression, no barriers between the arts, and no limits to the power of the creative arts therapies to help and to heal. In each of us, there is a well of silent music, invisible art, frozen movement and fantasized actions waiting to be brought to life.

Suggested Sources

Music Therapy

American Music Therapy Association
(AMTA)
8455 Colesville Rd., Suite 1000
Silver Spring, MD 20910
Telephone: (301) 589-3300
Fax: (301) 589-5175

Journal of Music Therapy
Music Therapy Perspectives
8455 Colesville Rd., Suite 1000
Silver Spring, MD 20910

Psychodrama

American Society for Group Psychotherapy
and Psychodrama (ASGPP)
301 N. Harrison, #508
Princeton, NJ 08540
Telephone: (609) 452-1339

The International Journal of Action
Methods, Psychodrama, Skill
Training and Role-Playing
301 N. Harrison, #508
Princeton, NJ 08540

Music and Imagery

The Bonny Foundation
2020 Simmons Road
Salina, KS 67401
Telephone: (913) 827-1497
Fax: (913) 827-5706

Books on Music Therapy and Related Topics

MMB Music, Inc.
Contemporary Arts Building
3526 Washington Ave.
Saint Louis, MO 63103-1019
Telephone: (314) 531-9635, (800) 543-3771 (USA/Canada)
Fax: (314) 531-8384, E-mail: mmbmusic@mmbmusic.com

Multidisciplinary Periodicals

The Arts in Psychotherapy
Elsevier Science, Inc.
Pergamon Press
655 Avenue of the Americas
New York, NY 10010
Telephone: (212) 989-5800

The International Journal of Arts Medicine
MMB Music, Inc.
Contemporary Arts Building
3526 Washington Ave.
Saint Louis, MO 63103-1019
Telephone: (314) 531-9635, (800) 543-3771 (USA/Canada)
Fax: (314) 531-8384, E-mail: mmbmusic@mmbmusic.com

References

Preface

Bingham, F. M. (1970, February). Masks as a psychotherapeutic modality. *Journal of American Osteopathic Association, 69,* 549–555.

Kenny, C. (1976). Video. *Listen to the music makers.* National Film Board of Vancouver.

Moreno, J. L. (1964). *Psychodrama, 1,* 277–314. Beacon, NY: Beacon House.

Chapter 1

Aldridge, D. (1996). *Music therapy research and practice in medicine* (p. 26). London: Jessica Kingsley Publishers.

Blatner, A. (1988). *Acting-in: Practical applications of psychodramatic methods* (p. 7). New York: Springer Publishing Co.

Bruscia, K. (1989). *Defining music therapy* (p. 174). Spring City, PA: Spring House Books.

Condon, W. (1980). The relation of interactional synchrony to cognitive and emotional processes. In M. Qui (Ed.), *The relationship of verbal and non-verbal communication.* The Hague: Mouton.

Morley, J. (1981). Music and neurology. *Clinical and Experimental Neurology, 17,* 18.

Priestley, M. (1985). *Music therapy in action* (2nd ed., p. 32). Saint Louis, MO: MMB Music.

Chapter 2

Moreno, J. L. (1964). *Psychodrama, 1,* 277–314. Beacon, NY: Beacon House.

Chapter 3

Nordoff, P., & Robbins, C. (1977). *Creative music therapy.* New York: The John Day Co.

Salas, J. (1996). *Improvising real life: Personal story in playback theatre* (2nd ed.). Dubuque, IA: Kendall, Hunt Publishing Company.

Chapter 4

Priestley, M. (1985). *Music therapy in action* (2nd ed., p. 32). Saint Louis, MO: MMB Music.

Chapter 5

Rider, M. (1987). Treating chronic disease and pain with music-mediated imagery. *The Arts in Psychotherapy, 14,* 113–120.

Chapter 6

Eliade, M. (1974). *Shamanism: Archaic techniques of ecstasy* (Bollingen Series, no. 76). Princeton, NJ: Princeton University Press.

Chapter 7

Bonny, H. L., & Savary, L. M. (1973). *Music and your mind.* New York: Harper and Row.

Bonny, H. L., & Tonsill, R. B. (1977). Music therapy: A legal high. In G. F. Waldorf (Ed.), *Counseling therapies and the addictive client.* Baltimore: University of Maryland.

Summer, L. (1988). *Guided imagery and music in the institutional setting* (pp. 11–16). Saint Louis, MO: MMB Music.

Chapter 8

Nordoff, P., & Robbins, C. (1977). *Creative music therapy.* New York: The John Day Co.

Chapter 10

Priestley, M. (1985). *Music therapy in action* (2nd ed., p. 99). Saint Louis, MO: MMB Music.

Chapter 11

Bingham, F. M. (1970, February). Masks as a psychotherapeutic modality. *Journal of American Osteopathic Association, 69,* 549–555.

Blatner, A. (1988). *Acting-in: Practical applications of psychodramatic methods* (pp. 13–14, 83). New York: Springer Publishing Co.

Chace, M. (1945). Rhythm and movement as used in St. Elizabeth's Hospital. *Sociometry 81,* 481–483.

Dobkin de Rios, M. (1984). *Visionary vine: Hallucinogenic healing in the Peruvian Amazon* (p. 73). Prospect Heights, IL: Waveland Press.

Eliade, M. (1974). *Shamanism: Archaic techniques of ecstasy* (Bollingen Series no. 76, p. 84). Princeton: Princeton University Press.

Figge, H. H. (1989). Controlled spirit possession as a form of group therapy (the Umbanda religion of Brazil). In K. Petzer & P. Egibo (Eds.), *Clinical psychology in Africa* (pp. 448–449). Unani-Enugu, Nigeria: O. Chuka Printing Co.

Junod, H. A. (1913). The life of a South African tribe. (2 vols., pp. 438–443). Neufchatel: Imprimerie Ottinger Freres. In Rouget, E. (1985). *Music and trance: A theory of the relations between music and possession* (p. 82). Chicago: University of Chicago Press.

Kendall, L. (1996). Initiating performance: the story of Chini, a Korean shaman. In C. Laderman & M. Roseman (Eds.) *The performance of healing* (pp. 49–50). New York: Routledge.

Marshall, L. (1969). The medicine dance of the !Kung Bushman. *Africa 39*(4), 377–398.

Mercier, J. (1997). *Art that heals: The image as medicine in Ethiopia* (p. 46). New York: The Museum for African Art.

Moreno, J. J. (1980). Musical psychodrama. a new direction in music therapy. *Journal of Music Therapy 17*(1), 34–42.

———— (1985). Musical psychodrama in Paris. *Music Therapy Perspectives, 1*(4), 2–6.

———— (1991). Musical psychodrama in Naples. *The Arts in Psychotherapy, 18*, 331–339.

———— (1995a). Ethnomusic therapy: an interdisciplinary approach to music and healing. *The Arts in Psychotherapy 22*(4), 329–338.

———— (1995b). Candomblé: Afro-Brazilian ritual as therapy. In C. Kenny (Ed.), *Listening, playing, creating: Essays on the power of sound.* Albany: State University of New York Press.

Moreno, J. L. (1941). The words of the father. Beacon, NY: Beacon House.

———— (1953). *Who shall survive? Foundations of sociometry, group psychotherapy, and psychodrama* (2nd ed.). Beacon, NY: Beacon House.

———— (1964). *Psychodrama, 1,* 277–314. Beacon, NY: Beacon House.

Mulindi-King, L. C. (1990). Lecture presentation, Nairobi.

Rouget, E. (1985). *Music and trance: A theory of the relations between music and possession* (p. 55). Chicago: University of Chicago Press.

Schultes, R. E., & Raffouf, R. F. (1992). *Vine of the soul: Medicine men, their plants and rituals in the Colombian Amazonia.* Santa Fe, NM: Synergetic Press.

Sharp, L. A. (1993). *The possessed and dispossessed: Spirits, identity and power in a Madagascar migrant town* (pp. 122–123). Berkeley and Los Angeles: University of California Press.

Trupp, F. (1981). *The last Indians: South American's cultural heritage.* Worgl, Austria: Perlinger Verlag.

Chapter 12

Keenan, B. (1992). *An evil cradling* (Vintage ed., p. 78). London: Random House.

Moreno, J. J. (1999). Orpheus in hell: Music and therapy in the Holocaust. *The Arts in Psychotherapy, 26*(1), 3–14.